Mentoring in Mathematics Teaching

Edited by

Barbara Jaworski

and

Anne Watson

for

The Mathematical Association

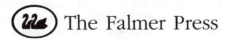 The Falmer Press

(A member of the Taylor & Francis Group)
London • Washington, DC

UK   The Falmer Press, 4 John St, London WC1N 2ET
USA   The Falmer Press, Taylor & Francis Inc., 1900 Frost Road, Suite 101, Bristol, PA 19007

First published 1994

A catalogue record of this publication is available from the British Library

ISBN 0 75070 258 3 cased
ISBN 0 75070 259 1 paper

Library of Congress Cataloging-in-Publication Data are available on request

Jacket design by Caroline Archer

Typeset in 10/12 pt Garamond by
Graphicraft Typesetters Ltd., Hong Kong

Printed in Great Britain by Burgess Science Press, Basingstoke on paper which has a specified pH value on final paper manufacture of not less than 7.5 and is therefore 'acid free'.

Contents

Preface   *vi*

Where to Start Reading

1   A Mentor's Eye View   1
    Anne Watson

2   A Focus on Learning to Teach   13
    Peter Gates

3   Mathematics and Mentoring   29
    Susan E. Sanders

4   Working Together: Roles and Relationships in the
    Mentoring Process   41
    Rita Nolder, Stephanie Smith and Jean Melrose

5   Reflective Practice   52
    Stephen Lerman

6   Planning for Learning   65
    Pat Perks and Stephanie Prestage

7   Interpreting the Mathematics Curriculum   83
    Doug French

8   The Wider Curriculum   96
    Barrie Galpin and Simon Haines

9   Evaluation and Judgment   110
    Maggie Crosson and Christine Shiu

10 Mentoring, Co-mentoring and the Inner Mentor   124
    Barbara Jaworski and Anne Watson

Notes on Contributors   *139*

Index   *142*

Preface

This book is written for teachers of mathematics at secondary level who work with students who are learning to become mathematics teachers. The act of working alongside a student-teacher in school is called 'mentoring', and a teacher who fulfils this role is called a 'mentor'. The book is written, on behalf of the Mathematical Association, by a group of people who are currently active in the teaching and learning of mathematics, and in the education of future mathematics teachers.

Why a Book on Mentoring?

As this book approaches publication, the arena in which the preparation of student-teachers for the teaching of mathematics is taking place is shifting its foundations and moving its boundaries. The whole basis of teacher education at secondary level is in flux with a move towards teacher education programmes which are largely school-based. This means some departure from established practices in which student-teachers spend substantial blocks of time in their Higher Education (HE) Department. The changes which this requires might be small or great depending on the nature of any particular teacher education programme.

However, there have been few programmes recently which did not place a significant emphasis on the role of schools and teachers in preparing student-teachers for teaching. A considerable move has been made in Great Britain towards programmes involving some degree of partnership between teacher education institutions and the schools in which teaching practice takes place. Where mathematics teaching is concerned this has involved relationships developing between mathematics tutors in an HE Department* and the school mathematics departments in which students have been placed. In many schools

---

* To avoid confusion between 'departments' HE Department (which refers to any awarding institution for teacher education) is always capitalized in the text.

a student-teacher has been particularly associated with one teacher in the school who acts as supervisor or 'mentor'. A mentor may or may not be a specialist in the same subject as the student.

A well-defined relationship between school and HE Department, with clear specification of the roles of mentor and tutor, is likely to form a good basis for a successful partnership. However, despite clarity of such specification, for those teachers who have not been familiar with working with student-teachers, the mentoring role may seem at best unclear and at worst threatening. What does it actually *mean* to 'mentor' a student effectively? What practicalities and issues are involved? What issues are there of which a mentor would need to be aware? How does this impinge on the role of the tutor from the HE Department? Are these roles separate or do they overlap? At a time of change for the teaching profession in general, and for the teaching of mathematics in particular, there seems to be a need for some elaboration of the nature of a mentoring role, and a discussion of issues which are involved in mentoring.

Why Address Mentoring in *Mathematics* Teaching?

The last decade, since publication of the Cockcroft Report in 1982, has seen a revolution in how the teaching of mathematics is viewed. It has moved through the introduction of GCSE, and its requirements for coursework, and has culminated in the Standing Orders for Mathematics in the National Curriculum. The related issues of classroom organization, teaching styles, assessment and national testing still rumble on.

There is debate as to whether the specification of hierarchies of mathematical content, through levels of attainment in the National Curriculum, is a step forwards or a step backwards in terms of the development of mathematics teaching. However, some recognition of recent advances in thinking about the teaching of mathematics is unavoidable. Pupils are to be encouraged to perceive the *power* of mathematics for communication and in its application to the world around us, to engage in practical and investigative activities, to make use of computers and calculators, to be effective problem-solvers and decision-makers. Popular views of mathematics itself, as a hard and boring subject despite its importance, have been recognized as detrimental to the effective teaching and learning of the subject, and national projects have been undertaken to change and improve this image. The aesthetic and creative aspects of mathematics are promoted alongside the utilitarian. The relative underachievement of girls in mathematics is widely recognized and teachers may take note of this in their expectations and teaching methods. Moreover, teachers are expected to teach mathematics within a multicultural society in which there should be equality of opportunity for all its participants, and in which contributions to mathematical thinking from non-western cultures are recognized and integrated.

Many of these changes have presented challenges and raised issues for teachers of considerable experience. They raise even greater challenges for initial teacher education.

Typically, the secondary teacher of mathematics has a mathematics or mathematically-related degree, followed by one year of teacher education gained on a PGCE (Post Graduate Certificate of Education) course.* On such a course, in the short space of one year, student-teachers have to be inducted into the craft of classroom teaching, made aware of all that is required of a classroom teacher, and enabled to recognize the issues for learning and teaching of the multifaceted scene described above. Moreover, they have to adapt their knowledge and perspective of mathematics and its teaching from that of recipient to that of provider. A high level of mathematical achievement is no guarantee of an ability to communicate mathematically at diverse levels, and may actually be a hindrance to understanding the mathematical perspectives of pupils with widely differing needs.

The teachers and tutors who provide the education course are crucial to the development of the student-teachers of mathematics. These people must themselves not only be knowledgeable of the scene and alert to the issues, but have a well-articulated sense of what it means for a person to develop as a teacher. For the tutors of an education course, these demands are not new, but they might be very new for teachers who, while highly skilled and experienced in school and classroom, have not been required to express or interpret their expertise for the benefit of other teacher-learners, or to take responsibility for these learners.

The partnership model of teacher education builds on the strengths of both teachers and tutors, recognizing that each bring particular experiences and skills to the job, and that these can be complementary and supportive. This book is written from a perspective of partnership. It assumes that both partners will have a commitment to the new teacher, and that a joint understanding of what is to be achieved and the potential complementarity of their roles will be an important starting point. The writing team includes both mentors and tutors.

This book tries both to encourage debate and to offer practical support to a new mentor. It aims to present aspects of the craft of teacher education of mathematics teachers, alongside a critical perspective of the issues, choices, and large or small questions involved.

An Outline of the Book

Each chapter is written independently of the others, and is the work of the named author or authors. However, the authors met as a team at various stages

---

* We recognize that there are other routes into the profession, such as four-year BEd courses, or articled or licensed teacher routes. All of these are currently becoming less common.

in the writing process to examine the content, philosophy and structure of the book as well as reading drafts and commenting on each others' chapters. The result, we hope, is a coherent presentation of ideas, with a common philosophy, which nevertheless preserves the individuality of the authors' interests and perspectives. There is some overlap from one chapter to another, and we hope that this is a strength in addressing issues from slightly different, although not inconsistent viewpoints. You could start to read the book in any chapter that interests you. References are given throughout to suggest where the chapters complement each other.

The Issue of Equal Opportunities

As editors we have tried to foster a sense of equal opportunity in the creation of this book. Each author's contribution and comments were valued. All had opportunity to share in developing the direction of the book. All authors are aware of the need for attention to giving equal opportunity to pupils and students in their work, and many of the strategies and philosophies in the book give implicit evidence of this. We have not attempted to make this explicit everywhere, nor have we confined the issue exclusively to Chapter 8. In editing the book we have taken conscious decisions about, for instance, the use of gender specific pronouns.

The term 'student' caused us some problems as it could refer to students learning mathematics in the classroom as well as to student-teachers, with potential confusion. For clarity we decided to follow the convention of referring to the former as *pupils*, and the latter as *students*.

Education versus Training

It is common parlance to speak of *teacher training*. However, we feel that the word *training* both strongly undervalues the development which is necessary in becoming a teacher, and also has perjorative undertones in terms of a 'formula' for teaching. Although the term 'training' is unavoidable in some of the official literature, we have tried to avoid it wherever possible within this book. We therefore employ terminologies such as teacher *education* and *novice* teachers.

Theory and Practice

It is inevitable, in handling a subject so complex as the education of mathematics teachers, that we present some very theoretical ideas, and some ideas which are more practical and designed to help the mentor get started. Mostly theory and practice are interwoven in the text, but some chapters veer towards the theoretical, others towards the more practical. After the Preface we present a diagrammatic view of the book which takes a theory–practice perspective and may be of help to you in deciding where to start reading.

The Chapters

Chapter 1 sets the scene with a 'mentor's eye view' of mentoring. Anne Watson reflects very personally on her own practice of mentoring, how she came to that practice, the principles which guide it, and the issues which it raises for her.

In Chapter 2, Peter Gates addresses the different focuses which influence a student-teacher's development as a teacher of mathematics. He considers the contributions made to this development by the mathematics mentor and the tutor (from the HE Department which offers the teacher education course) with particular attention to the learning processes involved. How can mentor and tutor make provision for this learning? What levels of support and challenge might be necessary?

It is in Chapter 3 that the special nature of mathematics and its relationship to the processes of teaching and of mentoring is particularly addressed. What *is* mathematics? What does it mean to *learn* mathematics? What does it mean to *teach* mathematics? How do teachers' personal philosophies crucially determine the way in which they work with pupils? What implications does this have for mentoring in mathematics teaching? Sue Sanders brings a blend of research and personal experience to bear in addressing these questions.

Chapter 4 continues and particularizes the theme of roles and relationships in the mentoring process. What are the responsibilities of a mentor? What are the ways in which a mentor can work with a student-teacher? How is it possible to provide a supportive environment, while still offering positive challenge? Rita Nolder, Stephanie Smith and Jean Melrose make extensive use of anecdotes from students, teachers and tutors to offer their perspective of various roles which can be manifested in the mentor–student relationship.

Stephen Lerman, in Chapter 5, takes up the notion of reflective practice and the part which this can play in developing teaching. He looks at the role of critical incidents as vehicles for raising issues which can lead to greater awareness of significant moments and a focus for classroom action. He develops the thesis that in fostering reflective practice through encouraging students to highlight their own critical incidents, mentors also enhance their own awareness of mathematics and its teaching. This joint raising of awareness feeds collegiality as mentor and student-teacher develop side by side, the mentor's own reflective practice acting as a role model for the student.

Chapter 6 takes the crucial task of lesson planning as its theme, and develops a model for planning based on reflective practice. Pat Perks and Stephanie Prestage address different elements of planning through a vision of planning as the basis for evaluation of a lesson, and therefore of initiating a critical approach to learning from lessons which are taught. The mentor's role in this is very much one of critical friend, encouraging the student to be explicit about objectives for a lesson and evaluating outcomes against objectives.

In Chapter 7, Doug French focuses explicitly on mathematics. While mathematics teaching has been implicit in all chapters, it is here that aspects of interpreting the mathematical curriculum in particular are addressed. What is involved for us as teachers in converting our own mathematical knowledge into activities through which pupils will themselves construct a rational mathematical perspective? How do we act in classrooms to enable and challenge pupils' constructions? How can a mentor provide experiences for students which will similarly enable students to construct their own perspectives of mathematics teaching? What are the issues involved, and how can student and mentor address these together?

In Chapter 8, Barrie Galpin and Simon Haines step sideways from overtly mathematical considerations to look at some of the wider issues in learning and teaching. A major focus is equal opportunities—in particular gender and multicultural issues are addressed. What relevance do these wider concerns have to the mathematics classroom? What about the whole curriculum? Pupils need to have experiences which cohere and fit with the whole school approach. How can mathematics teaching be related to teaching in other subject areas, and how are links made?

Chapter 9 is about assessment. Every teacher education course must have clearly designated forms of assessment, and mentors contribute to these. Maggie Crosson and Christine Shiu look at issues for the mentor involved in being supporter and critical friend on the one hand, and evaluator and assessor on the other. Of what does such evaluation and assessment consist? How can it be planned and prepared for? How is it possible to involve students in their own assessment? The chapter draws strongly on particular cases of student-teachers, their learning and its assessment.

The final chapter, Chapter 10, has two tasks. One is to draw together the threads of the book, and the other is to examine consequences of the mentoring role for continued development of the mentor and mathematics department through the mentoring process. Barbara Jaworski and Anne Watson suggest that mentoring can be extended to co-mentoring and what might be called the *inner mentor*. The first involves teachers actively working together to support each other and to further their own development. The second involves all teachers in developing a critical reflective awareness of their own practice and its development, which actively promotes further development.

It is on this note that the book comes to a close. The ultimate purpose of the development of mathematics teachers and teaching is the development of mathematical thinking and expertise in the pupils we teach. A question which we all need to address is, 'in what ways can the whole process of mentoring in its wider context contribute to the mathematical experience which we offer our pupils?'

Mentoring More Generally

We are aware of work which is ongoing in various institutions in researching the processes involved in mentoring student-teachers, not just in mathematics. For instance, our own experience owes much to the research and development work relating to the internship scheme operating through the University of Oxford. We provide several references below which offer further reading around the idea of mentoring in and beyond mathematics.

Finally . . .

We would like to thank Melissa Rodd and Kathleen Shaw for reading the entire text and commenting so meticulously. We appreciated the further insights which they gave us and the attention to errors we had missed.

Barbara Jaworski and Anne Watson
August 1993

References

COCKCROFT, W.H. (1982) *Mathematics Counts*, London, HMSO.

HAGGARTY, L.M. (1992) 'Investigating a new approach to mathematics teacher education: An action-research study', unpublished DPhil thesis, University of Oxford.

HARVARD, G. and DUNNE, R. (1992) 'The role of the mentor in developing teacher competence', *Westminster Studies in Education*, 15.

McINTYRE, D., HAGGER, H. and WILKIN, M. (Eds) (1993) *Mentoring: Perspectives on School-based Teacher Education*, London, Kogan Page.

WILKIN, M. (Ed.) (1992) *Mentoring in Schools*, London, Kogan Page.

Where to Start Reading

The numbers below refer to the ten chapters of this book, with a brief synopsis of each. They are arranged on a rough theory–practice continuum to give a sense of their emphases. It is possible to start reading at any chapter. Some readers will wish to work from theory to practice; others will wish to start with something more practical. This rough guide is intended to help you decide where to begin.

Practice **Theory**

←——————————————————————————————————→

1 A general perspective
  of mentoring

    2 Focuses in a
      student's
      development.
      Roles of mentor
      and tutor

            3 Belief or
              philosophy of
              mathematics and
              its learning—
              how this might

4 Roles of the mentor
  and relationships
  between mentors and
  students

              affect teaching

    5 Reflective
      teaching and
      ways of

6 Planning and
  evaluating lessons
      developing it

7 Interpreting the
  mathematics
  curriculum

    8 Issues in the
      wider

9 Assessment and
  evaluation of student-
  teachers' teaching
      curriculum

             10 The further
                 development of
                 mentoring

Chapter 1

A Mentor's Eye View

Anne Watson

This introductory chapter offers a personal view of mentoring which
is intended to set the scene for the other chapters in this book.

I started teaching by imitating my favourite teacher. She used to wait for quiet,
write mathematical proofs on the board, ask us to copy them and then work
through some related problems. I soon discovered (about ten minutes into the
first lesson) that this did not work in a city comprehensive 'middle' set. Instead
I let them continue to work through the available system of workcards but
insisted that they should talk to me about their work. I listened and listened.
Every lesson became an opportunity to improve my understanding of learning
mathematics; every response gave me a chance to learn more about my job;
every pupil helped me learn about children. Developing beliefs and teaching
styles takes time.* Most teachers continue to develop and learn throughout
their working lives. I like new teachers to see learning to teach as an ongoing
process.

Mentoring

For the past few years I have been associated, both as a mentor and a head
of a mathematics department, with student-teachers through a partnership
scheme with my local HE Department. Students are attached to the school
in pairs for almost the whole year, giving me the opportunity to watch and
influence their development throughout the course. During this time of mentoring and working with students, other mentors and newly qualified teachers,
I have come to the view that my own practice as a teacher and manager
has gained as much from the process as that of anyone else involved in it.
Mentoring has helped me think about what teaching means, what mathematics

---

* Doug French writes more about teaching styles in Chapter 7 and Sue Sanders writes about
beliefs in Chapter 3.

means, and to think about how to run a department in a way which encourages all teachers to consider these questions. Gradually I have turned my thoughts into practical ways of working, not always with success at first, but with a growing sense of an underlying approach to education which influences my behaviour towards pupils, students, colleagues and others.

In this chapter I hope to explain how I now work with students, and why I work in this way. I do not offer it as a recipe to be adopted in its totality because it took me a while to get to this point and much of it springs from my own ideas about how people learn. However, I hope it will give the reader something to think about and react to. For instance, one strong theme which I recognize in my work is that parallels can be drawn between mentoring and teaching. Many of the issues I raise will be treated in more depth in later chapters.

What is Teaching?

Teaching is a complicated activity. It is hard to define because it can include a wide spectrum of behaviour which we would recognize as teaching. Sometimes it means that one person will relate facts to others or show them how to do something. Sometimes two people, a pupil and a teacher, will be working together on a problem and the teacher is usually the one with the technical or specialist knowledge. It could mean that one person creates a stimulating environment and allows others to explore it. Others may believe that teaching is about the provision of discipline and the transmission of an unambiguous body of knowledge.

It would be impossible for one person to tell another exactly how to teach; the skills involved vary from teacher to teacher. From our earliest years we are on the receiving end of various teaching skills from many of the adults in our lives, not just teachers. Our memories of these and our reactions to them are quite important when we begin to teach. We take those memories into the classroom because our own successes and failures have somehow led to our decision to become teachers. Our methods and style of teaching are influenced by our understanding of children and of how society is or how we would like it to be. Our beliefs about education and our beliefs about mathematics all come from our own histories. Somehow these memories and beliefs have to be turned into practice.

I do not expect memories of what worked for me to coincide with other people's ideas. However, I was disturbed by this passage in a newspaper:

> Mr. Tomkiss was an absolutely brilliant teacher. He made algebra and geometry seem fun and fascinating. For instance, if somebody had not treated both sides of an algebraic equation equally he would say, 'Boy, come out here. Take off your slipper.' Then he'd slipper him saying rhythmically, 'What you do to one side you always do to the

other.' It was a joke of course. Not corporal punishment. (Lord Porter, *TES*, 20 June 1992)

I do not know what I would have learned as a pupil from that situation. It led me to consider where my ideas of good teaching came from and that *good* teaching may mean something different to individual parents, pupils, students and teachers.

It seems to me that for teaching to be good it must address the needs of as many individual pupils as possible and be consistent and sustainable. My practice is supported and sustained by my beliefs about learning and my subject knowledge.

What is a Mentor?

In Chapter 4 Rita Nolder, Stephanie Smith and Jean Melrose describe the roles of a mentor in detail, but here I want to give an overview which shows how I fit my feelings about mentoring in with the rest of my work.

A mentor is a guide and support to others who are finding their way into the profession. I do not think of myself as someone who tells other people how to teach. I provide them with pupils and classrooms and colleagues with whom to practise their craft and I have to balance the needs of the pupils and the school with the needs of the student.

Very often in teaching we cannot see the results of our work. If I think back through my own life it is often the casual remark or the ephemeral situation which has enabled me to make sense of a broader view of something. This could also be true of mentoring but that does not mean that the job should be done randomly in the hope that something might rub off on the student. The ground has to be prepared before the casual remark can have an effect. Consequently, I believe that mentoring has to take place within a structure which ensures certain issues are confronted in an atmosphere which allows and supports personal growth. Many of these issues are subjects of later chapters in the book, for instance Peter Gates writes about the theory–practice interface in Chapter 2, but here I wish to talk about creating such an atmosphere.

As a mentor I have learnt that, although talking has its place, listening to students is most important. One way for them to learn is by trying to make sense of what happens in classrooms. I could give advice, describe my own practice and relate anecdotes but in the end it is from what *they* do and what happens because of it that they learn most. If I can create a listening atmosphere between us when we meet, it is easy to move to discussion of issues or interpretations of events. It is also easy to respond to the students' own concerns and encourage a sense of personal growth.

I like to show that it is worthwhile to be a teacher. I enjoy being with children, teaching them, being mathematical with them and the whole business of education. Those learning to teach should see enthusiasts at work. I try to talk about mathematics, share anecdotes about pupils and articulate by word or action my excitement about being in school.

It seems vital that a mentor should be someone who is aware of developing the practice of teaching and is therefore not a stranger to personal change. I have to be prepared to examine my own work and reflect upon it, either with a questioning student, a friend, a colleague or on my own. If the listening has worked well, a student can become my *critical friend* for a while. She or he could be asking me searching questions whose answers cannot easily be found without some analysis of my practice. I may end up learning as much about the meaning of what I do as the student does. I do not feel threatened by this type of questioning because I do not consider myself to be a perfect or complete teacher in any way. The notion of having a critical friend is written about further in Chapters 4 and 10.

Another important ingredient of the atmosphere is trust. I believe that trust grows best through the shared task of developing the new teacher. The student has to trust the mentor to be an effective guide through the course and also to be a fair assessor. There is a deeper trust required too. Many students find teaching to be personally challenging in a way they did not expect. They may only be able to cope with their disasters and fears if they have a trusting relationship with the mentor. This can be built from the beginning of the relationship and I find it helps to show respect for students as adult learners who have a variety of past experiences and needs.

These overarching aspects of the work — trust, listening, enthusiasm and personal development — all take place in the context of a normal busy life at school in which the relationships between people have many dimensions. The pupils, parents, teachers, head of department, mentor, students, governors and so on all interrelate by making demands on each other and giving and needing support. The student brings extra pressures near the start of the year when teachers are fully stretched and least able to cope with their normal load. The pay-off does not come until much later when the student is able to contribute something back into school life in terms of ideas, special projects, time or extracurricular activities. How can the mentor balance all these needs?

Holding and Letting Go

I would like to offer some key words which describe an approach to all these relationships and help me bring them into a coherent network. When I reflect on the mentoring process I use these words to give a framework to my thoughts.

Holding describes a caring and supportive relationship in which there is metaphorical hugging going on. The hugging I think about is like that between a caring adult and a confused child. It provides a reliable source of help and guidance but at the same time puts limits around what is possible. It restrains but also reassures. The limits in mentoring may come from the ethos of the school, the planned curriculum, the disciplinary systems in place or the programme provided by the HE Department. I try to provide a combination of support, limits and a psychological homebase. I do not try to cushion students from the realities of the job or from the challenge of personal change. I cannot imagine how one could do this. In most schools the problems and stresses are only too apparent. The challenge is to turn these factors into issues about which one can formulate a view and hence build one's practice.

I am aware of a parallel between *holding* the student and my favourite teaching style in which I offer pupils a framework in terms of definitions and constraints and they work with some freedom within those. There is also a parallel with the pastoral role of teachers and the relationship between the pupils and their usual teacher, who may have been displaced by the student. Information about changes of teacher or changes in expectations should be given explicitly and maintained in order that no one should feel confused or threatened by changes due to the presence of a student. Pupils, students and colleagues should all know where they stand.

Letting go refers to knowing when and how to allow the student to take over sole responsibility for a class or for lesson-planning. I have to let go of my desire to check and influence everything. New pupil–teacher relationships will develop, new styles of teaching and learning may take place and it can be quite difficult for a teacher to let go of a class and for a mentor to let the student explore on her or his own. I have sometimes gritted my teeth outside the classroom door as 'all my good work' is 'overturned' inside only to find that 'my' pupils have responded very well to a new situation or different expectations.

Different ideas should be allowed to grow and be explored; discovery and risk should be allowed. I do not mean that the pupils' mathematics education or wider well-being should be put at risk but that students should be encouraged to try out unfamiliar techniques. They can push themselves to see what sort of classroom situations they can use which they may not have thought about for themselves. I try to ensure that they see a variety of teaching styles in action which might stimulate them to explore. I see experimentation as a part of learning because working entirely within what feels comfortable is unlikely to lead to growth or new knowledge.

Once I am satisfied that students think through the implications of what they have to offer, are aware of what goes on in their classrooms and can respond effectively to a variety of learning and behavioural situations then I may decide it is time to let go and allow students to find their own way forward.

Sometimes there may be differences between students and school which cannot be accommodated. Prejudicial behaviour or actions contrary to normal conduct of the school need to be tackled in a straightforward manner. It is useful to discuss the reasons for this, bearing in mind that our views are fashioned by our pasts. For instance, it is still possible to have student-teachers who have never worked on mathematics with someone of a different gender, colour or social background and who may act in an unhelpful way as a result. There is more about this issue in Chapter 8.

Differences of philosophy or beliefs about mathematics can, however, be tolerated and aired in an atmosphere of questioning and challenge. Conflict can force people to examine their rationale in the context of the shared task. Differences of opinion are not enough in themselves to delay the moment when the mentor lets go.

The Mentoring Environment

'Holding' and 'letting go' work if there is a structure which supports these ideas.

The Structure

I organize a regular weekly sacrosanct time to chat. This arrangement allows the holding relationship to develop. The meeting could sometimes have an agenda to which both parties can contribute along with others if appropriate. Adults do not always ask for time to talk if they need it. In fact, the more we fear we are making a mess of things the less likely we are to ask for help. I have to anticipate this difficulty and a fixed meeting time allows me to raise issues and ask questions during the good times and the not so good. The greatest pressure can come from a student's need for intermittent chats. This is a potentially stressful situation for me as the need may arise at a time when I have to rush to another lesson or have my own post-class incidents to deal with. Meanwhile the student may be in crisis. Generally breaks and lunchtimes can be used up with all sorts of concerns and I have to manage my own sense of balance as well as the student's.

Stress can be reduced by careful timetabling and also by spreading the load and involving the rest of the department in mentoring. My department is commited to regular review and development of practice and a spirit of mutual support and shared load exists most of the time. The business of listening to each other and discussing strategies is a normal part of work and the addition of students to such a department is seen as an enrichment rather than a burden. Students are included in department meetings as full participants as soon as possible and we often talk about how we are each teaching a topic or how we are encouraging our pupils to learn mathematics. We are all, in a sense, mentoring each other in the way we work together. (See Chapter 10 for a fuller exploration of this aspect of mentoring.)

Watching Each Other

Having students in the department has given us a framework for reflecting on our own practice. A colleague has said that the real test of how well the

mentoring has been done is whether students feel knowledgeable and confident enough to criticize the mentor's practice and how the mentor has reacted!
This would certainly be a good test but it is possibly more usual to expect
students to feel able to criticize their own practice in the spirit of reflective
development. Students have been known to sound negative in the early days
when they see things happening in another teacher's classroom which do not
conform to their view of teaching. I tackle this by suggesting that there are
some forms of questioning which lead to informative responses and other
forms which are not so useful. I try to turn questions which sound negative
into more neutral ones, but it is often the case that when a questioner focuses
on a particular incident the questioned automatically feels criticized. However,
'Why did you . . . ?' is more neutral than 'Don't you think you shouldn't
have . . . ?', for instance. When students question me, I have to be prepared to
respond honestly and that may include answers like 'I don't know' or 'It wasn't
very good was it; what do you think I should have done?'

I have found that a semiformal arrangement of observation is the most
fruitful and non-threatening way for students and teachers to work together.
There is some kind of agreement about what aspects of a lesson the observer
may wish to concentrate on and a feedback session afterwards which should
probably start with some kind of praise, moving from there to more contro-
versial issues. If the mentor is observing the student it is also a good idea to
say what went particularly well and not expect her or him to be aware of all
the good things. This also applies to the not so good things, but they can wait
until later in the conversation. A school I once worked in ran a scheme for
practising teachers of different disciplines to observe each other's work. It was
called Mutual Observation but quickly earned the nickname Mutual Admiration. Much of the mentor's task is to build confidence and a little admiration
may be worthwhile.

Discipline

Teaching mathematics and *discipline* are sometimes seen as two separate
issues. Although it is discipline which often causes anxiety and problems for
the student, particularly in the early part of the course, I do not see them as
separate and prefer to tackle both through an examination of the needs of
pupils. Students might be encouraged to consider that gearing the curriculum
towards the individual pupil might go some way towards building a good
relationship with a class so that many of the disciplinary aspects fall into place.
There are times when a more direct approach is required, but the idea that
good order in a classroom is about appropriate teaching is something which
students often find quite enlightening. There is a further passage on this in
Chapter 6.

Why Don't They Understand?

A more important question than that of discipline, to my mind, is one of which students may be completely unaware when they start to teach: 'Why don't pupils understand mathematics when I explain it to them?'

The realization that explaining something does not necessarily mean it has been understood usually comes at a stage when students are nervous anyway — the job is so new and multifaceted. Suddenly students, who have probably not experienced much personal failure in mathematics at school level, discover how little they understand about the learning process and how little they can assume about pupils' knowledge. Typically they are 'shell-shocked' by this discovery and may lose their bearings. What they thought teaching mathematics would be like turns out to be unrealistic. Their patient explanation, with examples, falls on deaf ears. They overestimate what pupils will know and underestimate the complexity of a concept they regard as simple. I say something like 'Yes, we have all felt like this at some stage and I still feel this from time to time', and try to get them to see that this is a moment to reflect on their own learning, perhaps on something they found difficult, or their views of what mathematics is or how it might seem to the pupils.

It is possible that students will discover they know less about elementary mathematics than they thought. They may have to pick their knowledge apart to discover assumptions and linkages of which they had been unaware. I continue to be surprised by pupils' responses even after many years' teaching.

It is a good moment for the student to ask:

* What is mathematics?
* How did I come to be able to do it?
* Where is mathematics to be found?
* How do I think while I do it?
* What am I thinking while I do it?
* What did I need to know to get started?

Some of these questions are discussed in Chapter 3. Whatever the answers, they find out that being friendly, knowing the subject and wanting to be helpful are not enough to keep a class attentive, usefully occupied and learning.

Giving Help

When trying out their practice in the early days it can be hard for students to take advice directly, particularly if the lesson had taken a long time to plan or appeared to fit perfectly with their treasured notions of the classroom. It can be hard to find the right advice. If things have gone wrong it helps to concentrate on a particular incident and ask the student to provide a full description of it first. It may be possible to describe it from several points of view. Within the descriptions there will be judgments made by all concerned about what was going on. Most of the time I have found that these judgments indicate beliefs and interpretations which, given time and discussion, can develop or change to give a different view. Usually such an analysis will result in an interpretation of events which offers a way ahead.

Sometimes students ask directly for advice about teaching techniques. I often find I cannot give my techniques because they may not easily graft onto another's practice. I couch my response in terms of my own teaching and how I make sense of things. I see my practice as a linked whole so that questions about discipline have to fit into my ideas about what a classroom should be like and how mathematics can best be learned. I try to offer examples or anecdotes rather than advice, but I cannot avoid this sometimes being interpreted as 'telling them the way to do it'. However, I think that I am offering a conversation in which the issue can be worked out rather than a recipe for success.

The parallel here is between mentoring and my own mathematics teaching in which I am often found saying 'Why?' and 'Tell me about what you are doing' and 'Talk to me'. This provides an opportunity for pupils to work things out for themselves though there are also times when I tell them things which help them move forward or refer them to other resources or people for help.

In mentoring mathematics teachers, just as in mathematics teaching, there are times when I end up thinking that a student is plainly wrong or heading for danger. The relationship is between adults so a way should be found to say clearly why something is inadvisable or wrong without too much distress. The holding aspect of the relationship may be interpreted here as giving firm guidance rather than reassurance. Sometimes the prevailing view in the department has to be imposed because my first duty is to the pupils and their experience must be coherent. An example of this might be an attempt by a student to give numerical marks for a piece of work when we normally give a written response containing praise, advice and encouragement. Another might be a student permitting food to be consumed during a lesson for well-thought-out ideological reasons whereas the school has a clear policy about the use of a classroom only as a workplace. Letting go can lead to a clash with normal practice as the mentor relinquishes control.

Some classroom situations which feel catastrophic at the time seem less so when the participants have more knowledge about each other. A shared reflective analysis, examining several different views of the situation, can turn the 'disaster' into a learning situation. The student is a learner and the pupil is a learner. If they clash it helps to be able to match up their stories. These can be stories about what mathematics is, or how it can be learnt, or about what it feels like to be learning something new. The mentor who knows the pupils and the student as people is better placed to offer ways forward than one who tries to deal with the situation without personal insight. If I can help a student to understand why a pupil is behaving in a particular way then we can move on to discuss ways to defuse situations, predicting what might go wrong and taking avoiding action.

The way I do this will vary from student to student. For example, a student who had just spent a year working in a home for maladjusted adolescents responded to difficulties with students in the classroom in a more therapeutic way than one whose previous experience was boarding school and Oxbridge and whose tendency was more authoritarian. I can see parallels with my teaching here. I do not expect all pupils to respond in the same way to the same situation. This does not mean that I move goalposts, whether they are about mathematics or behaviour. It merely recognizes that there are many ways to reach similar endpoints and I know more about those ways if I know more about the people involved.

If a clash happens between student and pupil and I have to go into a class to deal with it, I have to be aware that it could mean loss of face for the student unless I handle it carefully. It is quite easy for us to do this, and for its supportive nature to be understood, because in our department the accepted *status quo* is that teachers can wander in and out of each others' classes for a variety of reasons. Indeed we find this a useful way to share ideas. We like to be in earshot, real and metaphorical, of each other. The student can comfortably fit into a system in which intervention is part of how teachers value and support each other with sensitivity.

The Value of Mentoring in Mathematics Teaching

The mentoring process offers an intensive opportunity to develop the philosophy and practice of teaching for all concerned. Mathematics teaching is a particularly interesting field in which to mentor because schools can exhibit vastly different styles of teaching and make contrasting demands on teachers. In some classes the teacher is a remediator for pupils who cannot understand the textbook. This requires a rich collection of techniques and explanations available at a moment's notice. In others the teacher has a significant secretarial job to do keeping track of a scheme and equipment as well as offering further explanation, opportunities for conversation and so on. In others the teacher provides all the starting points and has to have all kinds of ideas for extensions or possible outcomes at the ready.

All these scenarios provide different challenges, as do the school's arrangements for setting. There are a significant minority of schools, of which mine is one, in which classes for mathematics are not set and students should be aware of the variety of techniques used in this situation. I have to steer the student away from any assumptions about a notional middle-ability and into the more exciting area of identifying common processes in mathematics. For instance, questions like 'Do they all know how to do simple probability?' are out of place but 'What methods have they met of recording and analyzing their results?' could provide useful information for lesson-planning.

One school and one style, while providing the holding structure and a place to work things out, may not give a wide enough experience of the issues surrounding education as a whole and the learning of mathematics in particular. For instance, any student coming to my school discovers that a pupil with language or reading difficulties does not necessarily have problems with mathematics. This makes lesson-planning a challenge but forces awareness of many other issues relating to models of learning.

Another issue which may be approached in different ways by different schools is whether mathematics has to be learned in a particular order. In our school we regard learning not as filling a cup but as a successful struggle with not knowing. Hence mathematics is not delivered in a particular order but by offering pupils a sequence of situations in which they could learn a variety of mathematics. (The HE Department provides opportunities to compare experiences with students at other schools and consider them in the context of wider issues and scenarios.)

This view makes mentoring very satisfying because the student's struggle with 'not knowing' how to teach is mirrored in the pupils' struggle with 'not knowing' mathematics. Information about how to teach is not delivered or absorbed in a particular order but is about response to a sequence of situations which really happen! A further satisfaction I find in mentoring is to see the pupils succeeding and watch the students realize that they were responsible.

Another fulfilling aspect of mentoring is a more selfish one. Having students working intensively with us forces us to reflect on our own practice and therefore makes us better teachers too.

'I noticed', said Meryl, a student in my classroom, 'how you lowered your voice when you wanted their attention'. I was delighted with this observation because I had been made aware of the power of this technique by watching a previous student use it two years before!

Nevil, a student in his first month of teaching, told me how he had asked another teacher to show him how to approach a group of girls, whose names he did not know, with a view to getting them to stop chatting. The teacher had 'wheeled around' the table to signal her imminent intervention, giving them time to adjust their behaviour, and gently stood behind them and asked them to talk to her about their mathematics. I had not thought consciously about ways to approach pupils before and the perception and sensitivity of the student had given me a new technique to use.

Susanna used a huge numberline from 0 to 1 and asked pupils to stick pieces of paper on it on which were written events whose probabilities, she hoped, were connected with their position on the line. Within a fortnight the whole department had used this approach.

Tom made contact with some difficult pupils by learning their names at the first opportunity and using them frequently. This is one of the important small things about teaching which we know are important but sometimes we lose our awareness and need reminding.

The presence of students helps to remind us of the important things.

Chapter 2

A Focus on Learning to Teach

Peter Gates

This chapter addresses what it means to learn to teach and to support this process as a mentor to student-teachers. It discusses the varying focuses of student-teachers during their education course, emphasizing the complementary roles of mentor and tutor in supporting these focuses.

Introduction

The Diverse Roles in Supporting Teacher Learning

In this chapter, I want to look at how student-teachers seem to begin the process of learning to teach mathematics, and how this might help us to a clearer view of the way in which the school mentor and the higher education (HE) tutor can work together. Teaching, whether it is teaching mathematics or any other curriculum area, is not just about passing on one's own knowledge to others — though this may have a part to play. In just the same way learning to teach is not just a matter of picking up some of the basic skills of classroom management along with a few good classroom activities.

The nature of some initial teacher education in the past saw the teachers in the school and the HE tutor working largely in (sometimes glorious) isolation. The teachers in the school with whom the student worked may not have had a clear picture of the student's course. The tutor may have had little real contact with the school department and therefore little influence or involvement over what experiences the student encountered during the periods of school teaching practice. Consequently, folklore and clichés abounded. Who has not come across the following views in some form or another?

- the HE tutors had 'airy-fairy' ideas divorced from the reality of the classroom;
- students were encouraged to forget what they learned in college as they were about to enter the real world;

- schools were socializing institutions which served to do little else than pass on outdated ideas about teaching and learning to new teachers.

Such a conflict of attitudes, ideas and interests can hardly be constructive, especially when the student is in the middle trying to make sense of it all. Happily, with the increasing collaboration between schools and HE Departments in the preparation of student-teachers, such a polarization of views is becoming a thing of the past. It is now recognized that both the school and the HE Department have a crucial role to play in the professional development of student-teachers and it is important to see the distinctive nature of these roles. This in part is what this chapter, and this book, is about.

It is not uncommon to hear student-teachers describing their periods of teaching practice as the most valuable element of their preparation for teaching. While students generally value the time they spend in the HE Department with their contemporaries, when asked how they think one learns to teach, typical replies might consist of, 'you can only learn to teach by doing it', or 'you learn it in the classroom'. Although this view is understandable, it is simplistic. It can encourage students to believe that learning to teach is a gradual accumulation of hints, 'tips for teachers', which they merely have to apply once they get into the classroom.

Learning to teach is not as easy as that, as those of us who teach can easily testify, and typically student-teachers are unprepared for the complexity of the process they undergo. Many students begin a course in initial teacher education expecting to be told *how* to teach so that teaching practice becomes seen by them as just an opportunity to practise those skills and techniques they have been shown. While the practising and acquiring of teaching skills and techniques is an important element in learning to teach, such a view overlooks the very real and often deep personal change required. It also, diminishes the significance of the school mentor to that of just being a model of classroom practice — a model which has the student 'sitting by Nellie'!

Working with a Student-Teacher

I believe that too much adherence to the view that learning to teach is mainly a process of acquiring specific classroom skills has influenced how some teachers have seen their role in initial teacher education. There is a wide disparity in how teachers work with students — which may have come about through a lack of communication between schools and HE Departments, forcing teachers to find their own feet and ways of working with students.

I will illustrate such a diversity of approaches through two hypothetical debriefings with a student-teacher. Consider Alan who is in the early stages of teaching practice. The lesson is Alan's first with the particular group of pupils and is on the relationship between the circumference and diameter of a circle. Alan provides the class with several round objects of different sizes and asks pupils to measure each with a piece of paper and to fill in a table with the column headings 'Circumference', 'Diameter' and 'C/D'.

First debriefing

Mentor: I thought for a first lesson it was quite good really. You already knew a few of the children's names which I think is important. But I thought you ought to have made your writing bigger on the board. At the start of the lesson you need to make sure that all the pupils are quiet and looking at you before you start. This always gives a good impression. While they were working they got a bit noisy. You will need to clamp down on that more or they will take advantage. You only had seven round objects for the class to measure which wasn't enough really was it? They had to keep swapping over with other groups which distracted some of them and gave them the chance to talk to their friends. I don't think this helped your discipline.

Second debriefing

Mentor: What were you trying to achieve in that lesson?
Alan: Well I wanted them to discover that pi was about three.
Mentor: How did you think they would do that?
Alan: Well by measuring the circumferences and diameters and then working out the last column in the table where they had to divide. They would see these were all about three. I got each group to give me the average of all their values to make it more accurate.
Mentor: Why did you want to do it in that way?
Alan: Because it is important that they discover things for themselves. It is no good me telling them that it's three. They won't learn that unless they have found out for themselves.
Mentor: So how the pupils explore, use and apply the mathematics is important for you?
Alan: Well yes. It is important for the pupils too if it is going to make sense to them!
Mentor: Can you tell me how Attainment Target 1 — Using and Applying Mathematics — figured in your planning of that lesson?
Alan: Erm. It didn't really.
Mentor: OK. AT1 is about pupils making their own decisions and conjectures and discoveries. What evidence have you that pupils were doing any of these?
Alan: Well by looking at the last column of the table they discovered that they were all about three.

While these extracts are not a complete debrief of the lesson, both are representative of how the conversations might have proceeded. It appears to me that the role of the first debriefing is to help Alan learn not only from his experience but from that of the mentor. In order to do this, advice and helpful suggestions about classroom management are offered along with other techniques to help Alan organize more successful lessons in future. In the second debriefing, the mentor seems to be adopting a more questioning stance, having Alan explore his own purposes for the lesson and the respective outcomes. Each debriefing represents a starkly different approach. But which is best — for Alan? How do we decide which is most appropriate at any one time?

I believe that tips on classroom management are very important — indeed student-teachers often seem to think they are more important than anything else they get from their teacher education course. However this approach seems to me to be limiting on two fronts. First it limits the student — in this case Alan — to having to take on someone else's knowledge about teaching (which was no doubt accumulated over years of being in the classroom) and second it limits the role the mentor can play in furthering the student's own professional development.

On the other hand, if this was an early teaching experience for Alan, the second debriefing may just be too challenging for him. He clearly says that he wants pupils to discover things for themselves, but he may not yet have a clear picture of how he might bring this about in the classroom. If his own experience has been of a rather traditional approach to the teaching of mathematics how is he to envisage a different approach? How should he begin the lesson? What questions should he ask pupils? When should he tell pupils things? Should pupils work in groups and if so how should this influence the task he sets them? Furthermore how must he keep their attention on the activity? Should the questions come from him or from the pupils? If he wants questions to come from the pupils, how does he go about encouraging them to pose their own questions? Is 'discovery' more than noticing a pattern in a table which pupils were instructed to fill in?

In a way Alan already has a somewhat enlightened view of how he wants pupils to learn mathematics, but as yet doesn't seem to know how to bring this about in the classroom. Learning to teach is such a complicated business, and it seems reasonable to assume that a very important and influential factor in this process is where student-teachers are in their own thinking about the teaching of mathematics.* How then are we to envisage the role of the mentor in this?

In the two examples above we might see the mentor as *offering* advice, suggestions and tips (as in the first debriefing) or *challenging* the student's awareness of their own practice (as in the second debriefing). A further strategy which might be fruitful in enhancing the mentor-student relationship is

---

* Barrie Galpin and Simon Haines, in Chapter 8, describe learning to teach as a journey. Sue Sanders, in Chapter 3, draws links between a teacher's own philosophy of mathematics and approach to teaching.

that of *probing* the student's thinking. A good way of starting in this way is with the request, 'tell me how you think that lesson went', or perhaps more precisely, 'Tell me what you thought went well in that lesson'. Such an approach opens up those areas which students themselves feel are important to them as well as giving the mentor some insight into what criteria the students are using for judging success in teaching.

It will be up to the professional judgment of the mentor to decide which approach to take when working with a student and this will depend largely on how the mentor perceives the professional learning needs of the student. It might be that probing needs to precede either offering or challenging. It might be that a particular student would find *challenge* potentially threatening and therefore unhelpful.

There are various areas of expertise that experienced teachers develop in order to carry out their work in the classroom, for example:

- classroom management skills;
- principles of classroom organization;
- broad purposes and principles of teaching;
- knowledge about pupils;
- knowledge about learning;
- knowledge about mathematics;
- knowledge of curriculum materials;
- ideas about teaching particular topics and themes;
- the school environment;
- aims and purposes of education.

This is not an exhaustive list, but shows how learning to teach needs to encompass a wide range of areas of knowledge and expertise. To become a successful teacher requires an awareness in each of these, at least, but also an appreciation of the links and connections which go between them. It's such a mind-blowing task, it's a wonder how anyone manages to teach at all!

It seems to me that there are two questions facing the mentor here. In what way ought one to work with student-teachers in order to help them develop professionally in these areas? And in what way ought one to work in partnership with the mathematics education tutor from the HE Department? I will consider these problems separately in the next two sections.

Focuses

Most teachers, of course, continue learning their craft throughout their career, but the most traumatic time is likely to be their initial learning. For pupils, there is a National Curriculum for Mathematics which organizes mathematical content into ten hierarchical levels. (There are many who would see this as a mistaken or simplistic view of mathematics learning.*) What of the process of

---

* See for example some of the contributors in Dowling and Noss (1990).

learning to teach mathematics — is there a series of stages or levels which might help us in identifying the needs of new entrants to the profession? Sadly (or happily depending on your point of view) there is as yet no suggested simple pathway, but there seem to be some common phases which students go through. At various stages of their professional learning, student-teachers have certain 'focuses of attention' which influence both their work in the classroom and their growth as teachers. The focuses of attention I would like to offer are:

1 a focus on themselves;
2 a focus on their teaching skills;
3 a focus on developing their teaching expertise.

There is of course a danger in describing such a process in that it can produce a prescription — a rigidly imposed curriculum for teacher education. All student-teachers are different and like pupils, have different needs. In Chapter 4 Rita Nolder, Stephanie Smith and Jean Melrose consider the variety of roles a mentor can take in the mentor–student relationship. As they point out, the decision as to which role to take will depend on the mentor's professional judgment based on an evaluation of the needs of the student. What I am attempting to do here is to present a framework, perhaps a rather crude framework, to help the mentor have some sense of where any student-teacher might be in their professional development. In particular I am suggesting that learning to teach, although a personal and idiosyncratic process, nevertheless seems to exhibit some trends.

So before I go on to discuss one way on which we might consider the process of learning to teach, I want to give a 'health warning': too rigid a view of the process of learning to teach can seriously restrict the student's growth! Exactly where each student will be at any particular moment, and the time spent at that stage, will depend on features particular to that student and to the circumstances of the school. However the roles which the mentor needs to take ought to recognize the potential for growth in each student, not being over or under-optimistic. The mentor roles are not a 'pick and mix' assortment, but rather a set of finely honed tools which need to be selected with care depending on the student and the circumstances.

Focusing on Self

Initially students often have a rather narrow view of the mathematics classroom in which teaching is about showing and demonstrating, pupils are seen not as individuals, but as a homogeneous audience, if indeed they are considered at all. Students frequently focus first on themselves and their own explanations and perceptions. Indeed it is perhaps because their previous experiences have left them with the strong belief that one learns mathematics first by being shown how and then by practising lots of examples that they actually believe that learning to teach is just the same process.

There is more to learning to teach than just 'doing it'. It is now well known that prior experiences and personal beliefs and values impose rigid constraints on the image of teaching mathematics which novice teachers bring with them to a teacher education course and that these images are very difficult to change.* The argument goes something like this: 'I have been to school and experienced first hand what it is like to be in a mathematics lesson. I was successful so the teaching methods I remember must be appropriate'. In a large-scale study of teachers in the United States in 1975, Dan Lortie found this pre-course perspective so significant in shaping the new teacher's subsequent practice that he termed it the 'extended apprenticeship period'.

There are however a number of dangers in the above argument. First we do not always remember as well as we think we do — especially when recalling childhood memories. Second, each one of us has only limited access to the mind of one pupil (oneself) and no access to the minds of the teachers who taught us. Third, the new teacher was probably a successful pupil (and most likely now has a degree) and is therefore unrepresentative of the school pupil population anyway. Fourth — and this will be more true for some than others — the teaching methods one experienced may be limited in their wider application. Finally how one believes one learned mathematics will be influenced by the view one has of the nature of mathematics itself. This is explored in greater detail by Sue Sanders in Chapter 3.

With their attention on themselves, students have difficulty seeing and analyzing much of what goes on in the classroom. Things are often seen as quite simple. The pupils weren't listening or working hard enough. The lesson went well because the pupils got on with the work. They fail to question what this work actually achieved.

Students often get lots of time to observe teachers at work, but complain that they quickly become bored and want to get on with some teaching. In short they do not know what to look for. We might therefore want to question the purpose of extended observation unless it is systematic and structured. When students begin their course they will have considerable (and perhaps in some cases entrenched) beliefs and attitudes *about* teaching. What they will lack is experience *of* teaching. The principal need is for students to question their previously accepted notions of teaching and learning. So it seems reasonable for the mentor to help the student reflect on these beliefs and attitudes while offering some insight into the mentor's own descriptions and understandings of the classroom. Perhaps the role of the mentor is akin to that of the guide[†] who takes us around historic monuments pointing out details we might have missed otherwise. This role might be achieved in a number of ways in the mentor's classroom in order to help the student refocus part of

---

* Evidence for this can be found in Leinhardt (1988) and in Calderhead and Robson (1991).
[†] Guiding is one of the mentoring roles discussed in Chapter 4.

their attention onto the nature of the teaching process and the nature of pupil learning.

For example, the mentor and student could discuss the planning the mentor undertook prior to the lesson and subsequently reflect after (or perhaps during) the lesson. The mentor could point out some aspects which the student seems not to have noticed in order to raise issues. (It is interesting that going through this process often helps mentors develop their own practice, as Anne Watson mentioned in Chapter 1.)

Furthermore, when it is felt appropriate, the student could work with individual pupils or small groups within the mentor's lesson. This might include:

- working with some pupils on the activity set by the mentor;
- undertaking a practical or investigative activity with a group of pupils;
- working with a pair of pupils at a computer;
- interviewing some pupils about their understanding of a particular mathematical concept or topic associated with the learning objectives of the mentor's lesson, for example, decimal or fraction notation.

Any of these activities could be usefully followed by a conversation between the student and the mentor, discussing what can be learned from what occurred.

Focusing on Teaching Skills

Another focus of attention for students is that of their own teaching skills in handling the classroom as a place for learning. Here the complexity of the classroom and the interactions therein are probably becoming more obvious to the student. There are particular teaching and organizational skills to be acquired and practised as well as skills in developing meaningful and respectful working relationships with pupils.

The role of the mentor begins to shift here to looking at the student's teaching. In a pre-lesson discussion attention can be on what it is the student wishes the pupils to learn:

- What are the learning objectives for the particular lesson?
- How exactly is the lesson going to start?
- What are you going to say?
- How is it going to proceed?
- How is it going to end?
- Is the activity going to be a suitable challenge for all pupils?

After the lesson the mentor can help the student to reflect on how it matched up to expectations, discussing what seemed to go well, what not so well and, perhaps more importantly, what are the criteria the student is using for making these judgments.* Sometimes a very useful strategy is to record one of the

---

* Pat Perks and Stephanie Prestage discuss these questions in Chapter 6 where planning and evaluation of lessons are addressed in depth.

student's lessons on either audio or video tape. This is a powerful way of helping students to 'see themselves as others see them'. With the support of the mentor, particular mannerisms may be identified, ways of speaking, standing, types of questions asked, responses made to pupils and pupils' reactions to these. It may be less threatening if the student is given the opportunity of watching or listening to the tape alone in the first instance, and then encouraged to lead the commenting.

It is at this stage that students begin to see how much work is involved in teaching and how little time there is to do it as well as they want. Because time is short, lesson evaluation is sacrificed to lesson preparation, and the student begins to coast along. This is a rather common feature of a student's development — reaching a 'basic' level of competence from which it is hard to recognize a need to change. Their lessons run relatively smoothly and they establish a set of successful routines. Progress begins to level out as students enter 'coping' mode. Their focus however is upon their own performance and how the pupils 'cope with the work'. Lessons are typically judged as successful if pupils enjoy them and could do the work that was set them. If students are to move on from this focus, they need to have their attention directed onto the pupils as learners *through* an activity rather than as a collected audience *for* the activity.

The pressures which may lead to the sacrifice of lesson evaluation can be discussed by the student and the mentor. It may be decided that time together is most usefully spent evaluating a lesson in order to keep the possibility of change in the forefront of the student's mind. The student will also need help in putting together lesson plans based around classroom activities. However, a mathematical activity is not a lesson in itself. It is the process of turning an activity into a learning experience — interpreting the activity in terms of its learning objectives — which now needs to exercise the student. This is where it becomes clearer that knowledge of the subject matter is in itself not enough in knowing how to teach mathematics. What a new teacher requires are strategies to turn *mathematics* into mathematical *experiences* for pupils; students need to explore ways of presenting and structuring certain topics and the opportunity to consider how well pupils make sense of the mathematics which underpins a specific classroom activity.

Interestingly, this process can help build the confidence of a student who may feel unsure about a particular topic. Many teachers of mathematics report that they do not feel they *fully* understood some aspects of certain topics, for example, algebra, matrix multiplication or probability, until they had to teach them.

Focusing on Developing Teaching

With this focus, the issues become more complex and in need of a more analytical approach. Students become more aware of cause and effect in their teaching — of how what they do can influence pupils and conversely how what pupils do can influence them. Searching and challenging questions begin to be posed. How do we know pupils are learning? What evidence is there? What is learning anyway and how do we bring it about? The student needs to face considerably more difficult issues which in part hinge on moral and ethical questions as well as on an awareness of various theories of learning. It may be that a student comes to differing views from those of the mentor. This could be a source of conflict, confrontation and impasse — or more usefully an opportunity for a mutual exploration of the issues, from which both parties may gain. This might be termed the *reflective* or *analytical* focus during which students may need to be confronted with their own practice and beliefs in order to take a more critical and analytical role.

If a student has commented that a lesson 'went well' (or badly), the mentor can help and support the student by asking more and more probing or challenging questions such as 'What do you mean by that?', 'Why did the lesson go well?' or 'go badly?', 'What might have contributed to this?', 'What other explanations might there be for that to have happened?'

The novice teacher may have to face potentially threatening and challenging issues. For example, a student may espouse views on *learning* which require pupils to be active explorers and investigators, making their own sense of the mathematical activities used in the classroom. On the other hand, the student's view of *mathematics* — perhaps resulting from strong images from their own experiences — may be that it is a fixed body of knowledge in which there are correct answers to problems given by the teacher. There is likely to be a potential conflict here which can show itself in a number of ways, most notably how the novice teacher interprets potentially open investigative activities and uses them in the classroom.

The anecdote of Alan, which I gave earlier, is a manifestation of this type of conflict suggesting that Alan needs to have his ideas challenged in order to move forward. The mentor could try to bring out a contradiction between what Alan admits to believing and what he does in the classroom. Whether or not this results in a change in Alan's planning will depend in part on whether he has a sense of what 'discovery' actually looks like and on whether he is ready to adopt this particular focus of attention. He may espouse values, but not yet be able to translate them into action due to lack of particular teaching skills within his repertoire. More importantly it depends upon whether or not students perceive for themselves that there is a problem or potential conflict. One view of learning suggests that we really only change when we are confronted with and recognize problems, conflicts and failure.* A mentor's probing can help such recognition.

---

* One writer puts it as: 'a thinking subject has no reason to change his or her way of thinking as long as there is no awareness of failure'. See von Glasersfeld (1991) pp. xii–xix.

Moving Around the Focuses

The more students I have worked with, the more I have come to realize that the three focuses I have suggested do not occur in a neat linear or hierarchical progression; students often seem to oscillate around the three. Indeed where some seem to be able to develop their own teaching by asking themselves searching questions when teaching one topic, there can be regression when asked to teach another. Perhaps the image of an unstable spiral is more helpful than a linear model. It is important for the mentor to identify the student's focus at any stage when deciding on appropriate support.

Links

There are many pertinent questions to be asked about the reasons behind moves toward more school-based initial teacher education. Most courses of initial teacher education have been considerably school-based for many years. Some would say the move was intended to make the education more relevant by making it more 'practical'; others see it as intended to remove the influence of HE Departments which the Conservative Government saw as being largely responsible for the widespread development of 'progressive' teaching methods. There is no doubt some validity in both of these arguments. However there is widespread recognition that initial teacher education needs a partnership approach in which schools and HE Departments work together to provide an environment and professional programme for the growth and development of effective teachers. Neither the schools nor the institutions can work alone and consequently what is now required is an appraisal of how that partnership can function.

Teachers have of course been working with students for decades — so in what way is 'mentoring' any different? The Council for the Accreditation of Teacher Education (CATE) has put it as follows:

> School-based training is not just extended teaching practice. It involves a fundamental change to the design, organisation and management of initial training. It requires a much more substantial and continuous contribution from teachers. (CATE, 1992, p. 2)

The change has to be a *qualitative* rather than just a *quantitative* change in the way teachers work with students and tutors; just having more teaching practice is not enough. The role teachers play will need to be reconsidered and it is likely that mentors will be more centrally involved at all stages of the course. Here I want to look at how the mentor and the institution tutor may work in harmony by recognizing the distinct but complementary roles they both have in the professional learning of student-teachers.

It is not just that the mentor works in 'real' classrooms, as opposed to the 'workshop' of the institution, which makes the partnership valuable for helping students to learn how to teach. Rather the mentor — like all teachers — works in particular classrooms, with particular children, teaching particular topics. These children have particular needs which have to be addressed, and classrooms and schools have particular circumstances which shape and influence what a teacher does. The school-based mentor would seem then to be in the best position to draw on particular classroom experiences and to help the student-teacher to make sense of them. HE tutors are not close enough to the classroom to carry out this task, nor are they able to be alongside the student frequently enough.

Of course different schools — and different teachers in the same school — have different ways of going about the teaching of mathematics. Some mathematics departments use an individualized work scheme for example, while others wouldn't touch one. Some schools group pupils in ability sets, while others use mixed ability groupings. New teachers need to be flexible in order to work in a variety of contexts after the period of school experience. Hence they need not only to have an understanding of the environment of the particular schools in which they carry out their practice, but also an appreciation of wider issues related to mathematics education in general.

Some of these issues are likely to be best tackled away from the immediate environment of the school. In Chapter 5 Stephen Lerman discusses the nature of 'reflective practice' — the capacity to stand back from one's teaching to consider one's own beliefs and values. Inherent in this is the need to have the opportunity to stand back from the school and immediate classroom environment and to take a more objective standpoint. This objectivity might be most usefully worked on when a student-teacher is able to meet with others working in different schools in order that experiences may be exchanged and explored without feeling too constrained to that particular environment.

HE tutors are likely to have more experience in the professional development of student-teachers than classroom teachers. They are more likely to be involved in professional development activities and more familiar with current research and development work in the area. This, after all, is their *raison d'être*. Furthermore the HE tutor will have an overview of a number of students, and will therefore be able to evaluate practices across a number of schools in a role as a moderator.

There is a further consequence of the mentoring role which could have wider implications for the notion of partnership. It is widely recognized that experienced teachers find it difficult to talk about the work they do in an explicit way. Much teacher knowledge is tacit or implicit and embedded in what they *do* rather than in what they are able to *say* about their teaching. This has been described as a teacher's *knowledge-in-action*. (For a more detailed discussion of this see Chapter 5.) One of the advantages of working with a student is that it can help teachers become more aware of their *own* practice and so contribute to their own professional development.

In the past the role of the tutor has been largely to work with the student-teacher in the classroom — perhaps replicating some of the work of the classroom teacher. A new role could emerge now which sees the tutor working much more with the mentor (and perhaps other classroom teachers) *and* the student. This will depend upon the way in which courses in different institutions are structured.

Tackling the Barriers in Learning to Teach

It is widely recognized that there are significant barriers to learning to teach mathematics. These stem from the image students have of mathematics and of how they conceptualize the role of the teacher and the learner in the classroom. Attempts to alter a teacher's approach to teaching will be largely unsuccessful unless the underlying beliefs are tackled. For reasons I have outlined earlier, students new to teaching tend to have a view of mathematics as a closed set of techniques which merely have to be demonstrated to children in order for them to learn.* Such ideas about the nature of mathematics and learning need to be challenged — but in a way in which the student can be supported. Sue Sanders discusses this further in Chapter 3. This revision of ideas might require some 'unlearning' by the student, and might be best carried out by groups of students at similar stages working together away from the school environment, which consequently seems to fall into the remit of the HE Department.

However this is not to say that the roles of the HE Department tutor and the school mentor are distinct in this respect. If the preparation the student receives is to be effective it needs to be consistent in the messages given. Challenging the notion students have of mathematics, for example, may require some attention at an early stage of the course in an environment which encourages change and reflection. It will also need to be supported and sustained in the school if such changes in a student's own attitudes are to be translated into classroom practice.

Learning from Experience in Learning to Teach

'Learning from our own experience' is a seductive phrase. However if learning is about changing our beliefs and behaviour, one thing we do not seem to learn from experience is how little we learn from our experiences! As T.S. Eliot wrote in *Four Quartets*, 'One may have the experience, but miss the meaning.' So while there might be widespread agreement on the advantages of making teacher preparation courses more 'school-based', if this is to be effective all those involved in it need to have an understanding of how or what is learned in this way — how people use experience to bring about their own learning, or in short, how to make sense of and get the meaning of the experience.

* See, for example, Ernest (1989).

What is required too, I believe, is a recognition of the constraints placed upon professional development by an overemphasis upon *experience* at the expense of *reflection* on that experience. Indeed one of the advantages of time spent in the HE Department during an initial teacher education course is that it gives student-teachers time away from schools to take stock of what they have experienced, to share their thoughts with other students and to benefit from a wider focus than an individual school can provide. Being able to learn from experience requires novice teachers to be given the opportunity of having time to identify and describe their experiences and thereafter to explore possible alternatives.

Much has been written about 'experiential learning'. One description of the process of learning through experience which I find useful in organizing my work with student-teachers is that given by Kolb (1976). This involves four cyclic stages:

- gaining actual experiences;
- observing and reflecting on those experiences;
- developing new ideas;
- experimenting with those new ideas.

This cycle can be helpful to the mentor as it gives some indication of the process through which the students may be guided in order to learn from their own experiences. In the classroom students need to move from the experience itself through to the development of new ways of thinking about that experience and then onto a change in their behaviour in the classroom. One approach to moving from experience to action which is often successful involves three stages:

- *returning to the experience itself* by having students describe particular incidents in as much detail as they can;
- *attending to their feelings* about the incident and trying to look for alternative explanations;
- *re-examining experience* in the light of these alternative explanations.*

However if this were just an internal process, involving the student alone, it could soon result in change and development being limited due to the narrow experience and expertise of the student-teacher. Here the mentor has the role of extending the student's thinking into new and potentially challenging areas.

One area in which this challenge is likely to be important is in identifying those occasions where there may be a disparity between what a novice says and what a novice is seen doing in the classroom. However, it is now being suggested that teaching requires a different form of knowledge than might be

---

* A fuller description of this process can be see in Boud, Keogh and Walker (1985). Further discussion may be found in Chapter 10.

experienced in, say, learning mathematics. Part of a teacher's expertise may be seen as embodied in what they can be seen to be doing — thus challenging the assumption that once we have learned something we can talk about it. There is much evidence that teachers' knowledge about their practice is 'tacit' — that they often find it very difficult to talk about even though they can be seen to be very good classroom practitioners.* This may cause some challenge for the mentors themselves in working to make their understanding of their own practice more explicit.

This offering of challenge has been found to be problematic in the mentor–student relationship. Research recently carried out in Australia suggests that some mentors do not wish to disrupt personal relationships by openly challenging the students' preconceptions. Yet this may be just what is required to facilitate learning in the student-teacher. Instead the relationship may be based in a largely oversupportive atmosphere.

One of the difficulties in becoming a mentor is in developing a new type of personal relationship in the school. Where previously relationships with adults in the school had been based on friendship or collegiality, when assuming a mentoring role they may need to be based more upon the need to create an effective learning environment for the student-teacher. While it is important for the relationship to be based on trust and negotiation, it is also important that the relationship allows for some destabilizing to happen within this supportive environment.

There is a fine balance here between challenge and support. There is some suggestion that it is only when both are high that novice teachers develop their knowledge and images of teaching.† Support without challenge may result in limited development. However, if the challenge is too high and support limited then this is perceived as threatening and the student fails to develop a constructive relationship from which professional growth is possible. Judging an appropriate balance might be seen as the mentor's responsibility, but if it could be the subject of discussion between mentor and student, this itself might form the most promising basis for a balance to be achieved.

References

Boud, D., Keogh, R. and Walker, D. (1985) *Reflection: Turning Experience into Action*, London, Kogan Page.

Calderhead, J. and Robson, M. (1991) 'Images of teaching: Student teachers' early conceptions of classroom practice', *Teaching and Teacher Education*, **7**, 1, pp. 1–8.

Council for the Accreditation of Teacher Education (CATE) (1992) *The Accreditation of Teacher Training under Circulars 9/92 (Department for Education, London) and 35/92 (Welsh Office, Cardiff) A Note of Guidance.*

Daloz, L.A. (1986) *Realizing the Transformational Power of Adult Learning Experiences*, London, Jossey-Bass.

* This argument is particularly well developed in Schon (1983). See also Chapter 5.
† See for example Daloz (1986).

DOWLING, P. and NOSS, R. (Eds) (1990) *Mathematics versus the National Curriculum*, London, Falmer Press.

ERNEST, P. (1989) 'The knowledge, beliefs and attitudes of the mathematics teacher: A model', *Journal of Education for Teaching*, **15**, 1, pp. 13–33.

KOLB, D.A. (1976) 'Management and the learning process', *California Management Review*, **18**, 3, pp. 21–31.

LEINHARDT, G. (1988) 'Situated knowledge and expertise in teaching' in Calderhead, J. (Ed.) *Teachers' Professional Learning*, London, Falmer Press.

LORTIE, D. (1975) *Schoolteacher*, Chicago, University of Chicago Press.

SCHON, D. (1983) *The Reflective Practitioner*, New York, Basic Books.

VON GLASERSFELD, E. (1991) *Radical Constructivism in Mathematics Education*, Dordrecht, Kluwer Academic Publishers.

Chapter 3

Mathematics and Mentoring

Susan E. Sanders

This chapter explores the view that the way teachers teach mathematics depends strongly on their own personal view of what mathematics is and how it is learned. It highlights some different perceptions of mathematics through particular examples of teachers' beliefs and considers how the beliefs affect their teaching. It suggests ways in which mentors can encourage student-teachers to become more aware of their own and other views of mathematics, learning and teaching.

Is Mentoring in Mathematics Different from Mentoring in General?

One's conceptions of what mathematics *is* affects one's conception of how it should be presented. One's manner of presenting it is an indication of what one believes to be most essential in it . . . The issue, then, is not, What is the best way to teach? but, *What is mathematics really about*? (Hersch, 1986, p. 13)

Why have we decided to write a book solely on mentoring in mathematics? Are the skills involved in mentoring a student-teacher of mathematics not identical to those involved in mentoring *any* student-teacher? Why give separate consideration to mathematics?

Readers will probably have a view about mathematics as a school subject based on their own learning experiences. As you read this book you will be aware that the teaching of mathematics can take a variety of forms. This is not just because theories about *how* people learn mathematics vary, but because there has been a wide debate as to the nature of mathematics within mathematics education circles.

In fact recently there has been debate as to what many subjects in the school curriculum really are. Is history about dates of battles and wars or is it about empathy with the participants? Is English merely about spelling and grammar? Is music only western and created by virtuosi? In many subjects this debate has been highlighted by the production of the National Curriculum documents.

What Different Views Might There Be?

My interest in what mathematics might be has developed over the last decade. I spent several years as an advisory teacher working with teachers in both secondary and primary schools. I was often asked to work with teachers to try out curriculum materials or ways of teaching mathematics. This is similar in many respects to a subject mentor's work. When I was a class teacher it had not really crossed my mind that teachers had different ideas as to what mathematics might be. As I chatted with teachers during the course of my advisory work I became aware that we were not always talking from the same viewpoint. I recall discussing subtraction with a teacher and suggesting that we asked the pupils *how* they had tried to find the answer to something like 412–187. The teacher looked at me in a somewhat puzzled way and replied that she did not think that was a good idea as she only wanted pupils to do such calculations 'using the right method'. I also remember another incident in which a teacher was not keen that a colleague and I allow pupils to draw any regular shape on the side of a right-angled triangle as an introduction to the theorem of Pythagoras. He thought it was much simpler just to tell them the theorem and let them do examples. He felt it would be a waste of time to explore anything other than 'the right shape' (i.e. a square).

These teachers were indicating that they felt that mathematics is about remembering methods that other people have developed. I feel mathematics includes creativity and intuition and wanted to demonstrate to the pupils that they could be involved in developing methods as well. These differing beliefs were stopping us from working fruitfully together. Similarly such differing beliefs could interfere with the work of mathematics teachers and student-teachers, and ultimately with pupils' learning.

Don't Teachers Always Mean the Same Thing?

It might be useful to consider for a moment other aspects of teaching in which we might assume that we all mean the same thing because we use the same word or phrase. Teachers often use terms such as 'good practice', 'child-centredness', 'group work' or 'investigational work'. You can probably think of examples when it became apparent that not everyone party to a discussion meant *exactly* the same thing.

During some recent classroom observation I discovered that teachers who said they were using 'group work' employed a wide spectrum of interpretations of that phrase. Priscilla had pupils on the same page of the textbook sitting around the same table but they were not allowed to discuss their work. Giti encouraged pupils to discuss their work in small groups before completing an exercise in their books. The groups in Belle's sixth form general studies class could choose a topic, women mathematicians for example, from a limited choice and all work to produce an individual report; whether they worked together, in pairs or as a whole group on researching the topic was up to them. Owen posed a question such as 'Which soap powder is the best value?' to the class of year 7 pupils and the individual groups had to produce a poster displaying their method as well as their findings. Perhaps you would come up with other ideas of what group work could be. From these examples it is possible to see that our interpretation of well known phrases is not as cut and dried as we might have first thought.

Finding Out About People's Views and Beliefs

I became aware that if my work with teachers was to improve I had to find out more about different people's views of mathematics. I did this in two main ways: by talking to and watching teachers at work and by reading.

When I questioned teachers about their planning I found that they took into account the age of the pupils and their ability, the curriculum or syllabus, the style they preferred to use when teaching, the way they liked to manage their classrooms and the materials that were available in their school. Although they did not cite it, I believe that there is another very fundamental influence on their mathematics planning. This is their philosophy of mathematics or more simply what they believe mathematics to be. As part of the same project teachers were asked what they thought mathematics was. (You might like to write down what you would have answered.)

However before I return to some of the teachers' answers I would like to mention some research into and writing about the philosophy of mathematics. Alba Gonzalez Thompson (1984) examined the practice and conceptions (beliefs, views and preferences) of three junior high school teachers in the USA, Jeanne, Kay and Lynn. She concluded that she had found differences in their prevailing views of mathematics, and that this related to their teaching of mathematics.

Jeanne viewed mathematics primarily as a coherent subject consisting of logically interrelated topics. She relied a lot on the use of mathematical symbols to explain things. She did not refer to the practical use of the mathematics but rather to how it connected with other pieces of mathematics. Neither did she encourage the use of intuition; she attributed poor performance to the failure to retain material taught earlier in the year. Kay, however, regarded mathematics primarily as a challenging subject whose essential processes were discovery and verification. She often commented on and shared the pupils' excitement when they made a discovery or gave insightful comments. Lynn's teaching and her comments 'reflected a view of mathematics as prescriptive in nature and consisting of a static collection of facts, methods and rules . . .' She did not encourage her pupils to enquire or find out for themselves; she preferred them to follow the procedure and get the right answer.

In classifying the philosophies of the three teachers outlined above, we might start by thinking about the following views of mathematics.

- *Logicism*, a view held by Bertrand Russell, is that all mathematical concepts can be ultimately reduced to logical concepts and all mathematical truths can be proved from these axioms alone;
- *Formalism*, a view held by James Hilbert, is that mathematics is a meaningless game played with marks on paper, following rules;
- *Platonism* (from Plato) is a view that mathematics is a static body of knowledge waiting to be discovered;
- *Fallibilism* is a view that mathematical knowledge is not absolute truth. It is open to correction and revision.

We might say that Jeanne's philsophy showed elements of *logicism*, Kay's elements of *fallibilism*, and Lynn's of *formalism*. This is however a very superficial analysis, and the above is intended to provide no more than a flavour of a complex area of study.*

Do All Teachers of Mathematics Share this Knowledge?

It may be that mathematics teachers and students training to be mathematics teachers have studied the philosophy of mathematics as part of their degree or have come across these ideas through a study of the history of mathematics. It may be that they have not considered them before. However they will no doubt recognize them as views of mathematics.

For example, you can probably think of a teacher from your own school days who made mathematics appear to be a meaningless game played on paper or with a heavy emphasis on rule following. I remember learning a subtraction method (algorithm) from a nun in which the moralistic phrase, 'and what do we do if we *borrow* girls? WE PAY BACK!' was a key rule. The notion that mathematics encourages logical thinking is widespread; many school mathematics policy documents contain the sentiment, 'Mathematics teaches pupils to think logically'. Many teachers may have come across the idea of *constructivism*, the idea that knowledge is actively constructed by the organizing subject and that coming to know is an adaptive process that organizes one's experiential world. This idea that learners construct their own reality and hence have to construct their own understanding of a subject has been influential in

---

* There is wide active interest in the philosophy of mathematics and mathematics education including an international network of researchers and authors. Some references are given at the end of the chapter. See particularly Ernest (1991). Details of the Philosophy of Mathematics Education Network are available from Dr P. Ernest, University of Exeter.

science and mathematics teaching. Teaching from a constructivist perspective requires teachers to be aware all the time that different pupils construct mathematical ideas in different ways, and that the sense they make is not necessarily what the teacher expects. What might this look like in practice?

Barbara Jaworski tells the following anecdote:

A pupil, Phil, was working on a KMP (Kent Mathematics Project) card involving finding areas of triangles. He called the teacher over at one point and expressed a dilemma. He had worked out the area of a particular triangle in two different ways and had obtained different answers. This could not be correct, yet he had checked his working in both cases and knew that he had not made a mistake. What was wrong?

Phil knew that *something* was wrong. Whatever method he used to find the area of the triangle, he believed that there could be only one result. He was very confident of his methods, and that he had applied them correctly. What should the teacher, therefore, do to help?

The teacher started by asking Phil to explain his methods, which Phil proceeded to do. The triangle in question had a right angle. One method was to convert the triangle into a rectangle, find the area of the rectangle and then halve this for the triangle. The other method was to square each of the two shorter sides of the triangle, add these together and then to find the square root. As Phil had claimed, all of his working was correct. And as he said, they should not give him different results.

The teacher's dilemma was how to get Phil to see that the mistake lay in his belief that both of these methods would give him the area of the triangle. [You will no doubt recognize that Phil's second method involved the so called *Pythagorean theorem* used to calculate the third and unknown side of a right-angled triangle]. The class had recently been working on the theorem of Pythagoras and the teacher realized that Phil's construction of the work on Pythagoras had been incomplete insofar as he believed that it related to the *area* of a triangle. The teacher could have told Phil that one method was correct and the other incorrect but he could not tell what effect that would have for Phil, who might not have been in any better position to make sense of the whole.

What the teacher decided to do was to remind Phil of the work they had been doing on Pythagoras, and then to get Phil to reconstruct for himself what the result represented (i.e. the length of the unknown side). Phil was then asked to contrast the two methods and to judge whether they would both give him the area of the triangle.

Of course the teacher could not know whether Phil's subsequent constructions were any more adequate than his previous ones. However the teacher had been given an insight into Phil's thinking. It is likely that this experience was valuable for Phil as he developed his thinking and his mathematical sense about triangles. (adapted from Jaworski, 1991)

This anecdote illustrates the different perspectives of teacher and pupil, and suggests that teaching includes responsibility for attempting to develop common meanings.

Some Teachers' Thoughts

To return to the question, 'what is mathematics?', which I asked of a number of teachers, what types of answers did the teachers give? Barry replied that mathematics was 'the ability to reason and see relationships'. Owen included the idea of mathematics as a tool for other areas of study. Priscilla said it was *useful* whereas Belle described it as *abstract* and not always applicable to real life. Bernard said that mathematics was something that enabled you to solve problems. Giti saw it as an intellectual challenge. (You may like to compare these responses with the interpretations of 'group work' from some of the same teachers, which were given earlier). A central question in my enquiry concerned *how* the teachers' beliefs about mathematics influenced their particular approaches to teaching.

Why Should Mentors and Students Discuss Views of Mathematics?

Once such differing views of mathematics are recognized, it seems clear that they need to be articulated in order for teachers to work together. It is not sufficient for teachers to assume that they share a common view. In the relationship between a mentor and a student-teacher, it must be important for the mentor to ensure that perspectives are discussed.

How Can Views of Mathematics be Discussed?

An interesting activity early on in a mentoring relationship might be to address following the questions:

- What is mathematics?
- What does it mean to learn mathematics?
- What does it mean to teach mathematics?

By probing and discussion both students and mentors should receive information about each other's views of teaching, learning and mathematics. Such an activity could be done individually or in a tutorial setting, perhaps also including the HE tutor.

Why Is It Important to Share Views?

I feel that a shared understanding of these three elements is very important in the student–mentor relationship because they influence so strongly what goes on in a classroom.

First, a teacher's view of mathematics could have differing effects on different pupils. For example two distinct learning strategies have been observed by Gordon Pask (1976), who suggests that different learners appear to be able to operate with different levels of uncertainty.

A *serialist* mode of learning is to move from certainty to certainty working with parcels of knowledge that are small, well defined and sequential. Learners prefer to work from certainty to certainty. One sure step at a time could well be their maxim. Teachers whose view of mathematics is predominantly *logicist* — that 1) all mathematical concepts can be ultimately reduced to logical concepts and 2) all mathematical truths can be proved from these axioms alone — might work well with a serialist learning pupil. That pupil could achieve well with the regular teacher because of their compatible views. The student-teacher might not see mathematics that way at all, which could cause the pupil's performance to decrease.

Pask's other mode of learning, the *holist* mode, involves working in an exploratory way, understanding the whole framework and filling in details by noticing relationships. Pupils in this mode might respond better to a teacher with a *fallibilist* or *constructivist* view of mathematics than one with, say, a *formalist* view. If the student-teacher and regular teacher have different views the pupil's performance, again, could be affected. In fact some learners exhibit both forms of learning and it appears that those with flexibility in style are more successful learners. (There is further discussion of this below.)

Second, it is important for mentors and student-teachers to consider beliefs about mathematics because the learner's own view of mathematics is influenced by the messages about mathematics that the teacher is sending out. Learners pick up with ease teachers' views and preferences in mathematics. Rosalinde Scott-Hodgetts (1986) reports the following incident:

Interviewer: What sort of maths do you think your teacher feels is important?

Susan (age 10): Um. The adding, and times and things like that. And she likes us to write it all out, the sum, and not think in our head and then write it: like three chickens — if three farmers had nine chickens, how many would they have each? Not three chickens — she'd want us to write it out: nine divided by three equals three chickens. We've got to write it out. Neatly.

Research into models of learning indicates that the more flexible the model(s) employed by teachers the more 'successful' the learning by the pupils. Research has found that mathematically able pupils demonstrate a versatility of approach.* In some problem solving situations a process that has been used before leads to a solution whereas in other situations past experience has to be restructured to fit the new situation.† Versatile learners are more able to judge what is appropriate.

I believe that it is also true that successful mathematicians need to employ different views of mathematics in different situations. Teachers of mathematics therefore also have to appreciate different views of mathematics. It is thus an important aspect of the mentor's role to encourage discussions between students intending to become mathematics teachers and experienced mathematics teachers about possible consequences of their differing views of mathematics.

Third, it is important for students and mentors to discuss beliefs and views about mathematics because the view of mathematics held by a teacher influences that teacher's teaching. This was well illustrated in Alba Gonzalez Thompson's (1984) study which shows the relationship of each teacher's conceptions (beliefs, views and preferences) of mathematics and her mathematics teaching.

For example, Jeanne saw mathematics as a coherent collection of interrelated concepts and procedures, a consistent subject free of ambiguity and arbitrariness. In her teaching she stressed the meaning of the concepts taught in terms of their relationship to other bits of mathematics. She viewed mathematical activities as some sort of game with symbols played according to rules. Not only did this influence the way she taught the mathematics content, it influenced the way she ran her classroom. She saw the role of the teacher to establish and maintain an atmosphere of order, respect and courtesy. She presented the content in a clear, logical and precise manner. She believed that the teacher should control and direct all instructional activities and have a clear plan for the lessons. She asked questions which were mainly intended to elicit short, simple answers and she had a tendency to disregard the students' suggestions and not to follow through their ideas.

Of course beliefs about mathematics are not the only things that influence the way teachers teach mathematics. Personal confidence with mathematics can be a considerable influence, as can considerations of behaviour and discipline, as Rita Nolder (1988) indicated, but these issues are beyond the scope of this chapter.

What Effects Might Different Views of Mathematics have in a Classroom Situation?

Let us consider the following fictitious mathematics lesson and look at it from several people's points of view.

---

* See, for example, Krutetskii (1976).
† See, for example, Birch and Rabinowitz (1968).

Mrs Williams

To begin with let us imagine Mrs Williams, an interested and concerned parent, the type who asks a pupil what they have done at school that day.

'We had maths with Ms Cockcroft', Ceri replies.

Now of course we all know how important mathematics is as a school subject so Mrs Williams probes. 'And what did you do in mathematics?' she asks, perhaps remembering her own mathematics lessons at that age, the diagram on the board, the explanation by the teacher and the ten examples to be done in the lesson and finished for homework.

'Oh we built walls with multilink bricks', Ceri replies.

Mrs Williams thinks she must have misunderstood. 'Multilink bricks, what are those?' she asks.

'A bit like Lego only they fit together on every side'.

Mrs Williams' mind races. Tabloid reports of falling standards, politicians' decrying trendy teachers, employers' statements of unemployable school leavers fill her consciousness. She prepares for a confrontation and telephones the school for an appointment.

Ms Cockcroft

The weekend before Ms Cockcroft had been carefully planning her week's work with 2-alpha. They are a bright group and she prefers to give them open ended work. She remembers an activity from an INSET course she attended last year. The video that they had been shown of pupils working with multilink cubes included plenty of lively discussion and the pupils were using a wide range of mathematical skills to explore the relationships. Yes, she would do the wall activity with 2-alpha on Monday afternoon.

Mr Durrell

Mr Durrell is doing his PGCE course at Bayside University. He is one of a group of students working at the Bridge School. On Monday he is working with Ms Cockcroft. They haven't had much time to discuss what she is doing as there was a staff meeting at lunch time and he had only just arrived in time for the start of school in the morning due to a mix-up over transport. He is relieved to find the they are doing the multilink wall activity as he has done that in college and he remembers the relationship between the number of bricks and the height of the wall. He finds a group of rather quiet girls looking at a pile of cubes. They haven't even started yet and several groups are building all sorts of walls. Yes, he can help this group.

'Start building walls', he encourages, 'and think about a formula with brackets and a division in'.

Ceri

Ceri is enjoying the mathematics lesson. Group work is OK if you're working with sensible people and today it has worked out well. They got organized before they started and everybody is building a different height wall and recording their results on a large sheet of sugar paper. The number pattern looks familiar but Ceri can't actually remember how to write the relationship as a formula.

Jo takes a lead: 'What shall we call the height of the wall?'

'Let's be really original and call it H' Ceri suggests. The group laughs.

Jo

In three years' time when they are taking their GCSE examinations Jo stares at the paper. There is a diagram of a tower constructed from cubes. 'Find the relationship between the height of the tower and the number of cubes in the base', the question asks. An image of Ms Cockcroft's lesson comes into Jo's mind; everyone is laughing. Why? Oh yes of course Ceri said . . . and Jo begins the question.

Well, it was the same lesson wasn't it? However, viewed from different perspectives it led to very different interpretations. Jo certainly learnt something. Mr Durrell had a different objective for his intervention than Ms Cockcroft would have had, while the lesson was not what Mrs Williams expected at all. Perhaps she understood when Ms Cockcroft explained her aims and objectives when she came to the school.

No doubt the parents of pupils in your school have the opportunity to find out about the way you teach mathematics and would not have been panic-stricken at the thought of a mathematics lesson where pupils play with plastic bricks. Any students welcomed into your classrooms will have been better briefed than Mr Durrell. But this imaginary lesson highlights how different views of what mathematics *is* coloured the adults' interpretations of that lesson.

What Should Mentors and Students Do?

However fleeting mathematics learning is, or however it happens, teachers have ideas of what they can realistically expect pupils to learn from an activity and a view of how they best learn. How do teachers articulate these ideas to the student-teachers with whom they are working?

What Could Mathematics Mentors Do?

- Mathematics mentors could think back to students or colleagues with whom they have worked. They could remember articles they have read or in-service courses on mathematics that they have attended. They could probably recall an instance of each when they were aware of having a view of mathematics, learning of mathematics or teaching of mathematics that was different from other people's views.

- What questions might they have asked in order to explore these differences?
- How crucial were the different views? Did they affect the outcome?
- Were they able to accept the other view, or did they refuse to consider the activity because the notion of mathematics was so different from their own?
- Did they waste time and energy because they had not fully understood the initial premise from which the other person was working?

Perhaps they would begin to see how important and efficient it would be to spend time on an exploration of students' views at the *beginning* of, and throughout, the mentoring relationship.

What Activities Could be Used with Students?

- Students could be given reading to do during the college-based part of the course.
- During observation, student-teachers could be asked to look for illustrations of particular views of mathematics from both pupils and teachers. These observations could be used to illustrate a discussion either in school or in the HE Department.
- Student-teachers could be asked to find a lesson either from a published scheme or from a teachers' journal such as *Mathematics in School* or *Mathematics Teaching* and to evaluate the view of mathematics it could give to a pupil.
- Mentors could discuss what they perceived a student-teacher's beliefs about mathematics to be from a lesson, and discuss whether or not their perception was really what the student-teacher believed.
- Student-teachers could be encouraged to include a consideration of beliefs about mathematics when planning work for failing pupils.
- Mentors could utilize comment in the media and from parents, politicians and others, to discuss beliefs about mathematics with fellow teachers and student-teachers perhaps as part of departmental professional development sessions.

Is Mentoring in Mathematics Different from Mentoring in General?

To return to the question I posed at the beginning of this chapter one of the aspects that I think make it necessary to deal with mentoring in mathematics separately from other subjects is that teachers have different views of what it is they are teaching and this influences their teaching. Thus discussion of views about mathematics is an important interchange between mentors and student-teachers and can strongly influence the success of the relationship.

References

BIRCH, H.G. and RABINOWITZ, H.S. (1968) 'The negative effects of previous experience on productive thinking' in WASON, P.C. and JOHNSON-LAIRD, P.N. (Eds) *Thinking and Reasoning,* London, Penguin.

ERNEST P. (1985) 'The philosophy of mathematics and mathematical education', *The International Journal of Mathematical Education in Science and Technology,* **16**, 5, pp. 603–12.

ERNEST, P. (1991) *Philosophy of Mathematics Education,* London, Falmer Press.

GONZALEZ THOMPSON, A. (1984) 'The relationship of teachers' conceptions of mathematics teaching to instructional practice', *Educational Studies in Mathematics,* **15**, pp. 105–27.

HERSCH, R. (1986) 'Some proposals for revising the philosophy of mathematics' in TYMOCZKO, T. (Ed.) *New Directions in the Philosophy of Mathematics,* Boston, Birkhauser.

JAWORSKI, B. (1988) ' "Is" versus "seeing as": Constructivism and the mathematics classroom' in PIMM, D. (Ed.) *Mathematics, Teachers and Children,* London, Hodder and Stoughton.

JAWORSKI, B. (1991) 'Interpretations of a constructivist philosophy in mathematics teaching', unpublished PhD thesis, Milton Keynes, Open University.

KRUTETSKII, V.A. (1976) *The Psychology of Mathematical Abilities in School Children,* Chicago, University of Chicago Press.

NOLDER, R. (1988) 'Responding to change' in PIMM, D. (Ed.) *Mathematics, Teachers and Children,* London, Hodder and Stoughton.

PASK, G. (1976) *The Cybernetics of Human Learning and Performance,* London, Hutchinson.

SCOTT-HODGETTS, R. (1986) 'Girls and mathematics: The negative implications of success' in BURTON, L. (Ed.) *Girls into Maths Can Go,* London, Holt, Rinehart and Winston.

Chapter 4

Working Together: Roles and Relationships in the Mentoring Process

Rita Nolder, Stephanie Smith and Jean Melrose

The success of mentoring depends strongly on the relationship which develops between the mentor and student-teachers. This chapter highlights a number of roles which the mentor can play as part of the relationship and raises issues very practically through case studies of particular students and mentors.

Introduction

It's important to set up the right sort of relationship in the first place so that if you wander into the classroom, students don't feel intimidated and don't see you as checking up on them. It's how you set up the relationship which matters. You have to work *with* the students.

This comment from Lucy, a mathematics teacher, who is responsible for mathematics student-teachers in an 11–18 comprehensive school, sets the scene for this chapter which focuses on the roles and relationships involved in the mentoring process. When students and teachers talk about the teaching practice experience, it becomes clear that the perceived success or failure of the experience hinges on the quality of the relationships formed and the expectations of both parties with regard to the roles to be played by students and supervising teachers.* While official documents and guidelines may describe what classroom teachers should do when supervising students and what roles they should play, these roles are bound up with relationships which are less tangible and impossible to legislate for. Of course these relationships are professional relationships and are developed in the context of managing the

* See, for example Southall and King (1979) and Hodgkinson (1992).

mathematics curriculum and making necessary links with the National Curriculum. The aim is to ensure that a good range and quality of experiences, with appropriate teaching styles and resources, is available for the pupils.

The purpose of this chapter, then, is to draw attention to and raise questions about the roles and relationships involved in the mentoring process, since an awareness of the issues, the *personal* as well as the *methodological*, is likely to be a critical factor influencing the teaching practice experience. We highlight some of the ways in which the mentor's role of trusted and experienced adviser, in all its complexity, can be viewed. These have been described as,

- supportive fellow professional:
- listening friend;
- supportive critic;
- gatekeeper and guide;
- link agent.

While not forming an exhaustive description of the mentor's task, they serve to illustrate the range of sensitivity and skill to be brought to this essentially enabling task (see also Chapters 1, 5 and 10). We shall refer to the work of four teachers who played a mentoring role for students, although *mentor* may not have been the title assigned to them. As stated before, Lucy is a mathematics teacher who is responsible for mathematics students in an 11–18 comprehensive school. Gill is the head of mathematics in an 11–16 comprehensive school and is Rachel's mentor. Barbara is the head of mathematics in a 11–18 comprehensive school and is Kevin's mentor. Shaheen is a mathematics teacher who has responsibility for all student-teachers in an 11–14 comprehensive school. In addition we draw on the comments of Paula (a tutor and teaching practice supervisor from an HE Department), Rachel, Liz, Vince, Kevin, Sarah, Sezu, and Emily (students) and Nick (in his first year of teaching).

Supportive Fellow Professional

First and perhaps foremost, the mentor is the student-teacher's *supporter* and *encourager*. To illustrate the complexity of this role we give two anecdotes, the first of Rachel, a student who experienced difficulty matching work to low attaining groups and the second of Kevin who built up a constructive relationship after losing his temper with a particularly awkward boy, and their respective mentors Gill and Barbara. We draw out from the anecdotes and the subsequent discussions some aspects of professional practice that were perceived as important by the mentor and student in their working together.

Rachel, an able mathematician, had a successful first teaching practice in a girls' independent school. Her final teaching practice, in a mixed 11–16 comprehensive school, brought her into contact with lower achieving pupils in a mixed ability setting. She had planned to do what seemed, to Gill, like a fortnight's work in her first session on angles with a year 7 class. The worksheet that she had made was appropriate for the most able group in the class and no one else.

Gill, the head of maths in the school, and Rachel's mentor, was sensitive to Rachel's inexperience and apprehension of preparing tasks for the wide range of pupils.* Gill pointed out some of the limitations she had found in the book the class normally used, saying for example: 'I would normally leave that out'. or 'You may need some easier questions before that exercise.'

She showed Rachel the resources available: angle measures, protractors (Rachel had assumed that the pupils would automatically provide their own), scissors, card ('it's expensive'), plastic plane shapes etc. Rachel was being encouraged, implicitly, to incorporate practical activities in her teaching and to exercise judgment about available resources. Rachel herself remembered software: a Microsmile program to help with estimating angles, the possibility of using LOGO.

Gill and Rachel worked together to plan an introduction to find out what the pupils could remember about angles from their primary school mathematics (whole turns, half turns, quarter turns, right angles, followed by pupils comparing the size of pairs of angles). Rachel wondered about introducing an anti-clockwise turn as positive; Gill was cautious, thinking of the work on bearings that was to come. The ideas that they had worked out together were successfully implemented by Rachel and their next discussion focused on the content and presentation of a worksheet for the lowest achieving group, and on the organization involved in using LOGO since the micros were located in the computer room which was some distance from their normal classroom.

Kevin, in his final long teaching practice, taught a class which included Andy, an able 12 year old who, along with generally messing around and being inattentive, was seriously underachieving. His relationship with his classmates was strained; they could easily 'wind him up' by teasing him about his father who was a teacher in the school. He seemed isolated.

Kevin found working with the class frustrating and things came to a head when Andy's behaviour and insolence had caused uproar. Kevin explained the situation and how it had arisen to Barbara, his mentor. He felt that he had lost his temper and mishandled the situation and was unsure of how to proceed.

Barbara and Kevin together decided on long-term strategies needed to address Andy's lack of success. In the short term Kevin explained to Andy that it might be beneficial for each of them to have a break from each other and asked him if he would like to work with a group of pupils in Barbara's class. He did so, and soon experienced success by finding he was able to contribute a good idea to help the group with which he was working. They were investigating the number of different sized squares within a large square and were

---

* Chapter 6 looks at this planning process in some detail.

having difficulty with the counting involved. So Andy suggested cutting out a square of paper and moving it along the larger grid.

Barbara and Kevin discussed Andy's progress a couple of weeks later. Kevin talked to Andy about the success he was showing now, in contrast to the lack of achievement he had previously found in his everyday mathematical work (in an individualized scheme). It was agreed that the level of his work within the scheme would be raised if Andy was prepared to discuss where he was having difficulty because of gaps in his knowledge, rather than using 'being stuck' as an opportunity to mess about. A level of personal responsibility had been induced in Andy; the strategy adopted by both Kevin and Barbara conveyed the message that he could be trusted; a new start for Andy had been negotiated and he was successful. In fact, he went on take A level mathematics. Kevin's negotiation with Andy extended his set of strategies, both in working with an awkward pupil and in collaborating with colleagues to enable that pupil to feel valued.

A key theme is that in each case the mentor and the student worked together to tackle a problem, each contributing to the discussion. Empathy is an essential quality for a mentor. Implicit in the ways in which Gill related to Rachel, and Barbara to Kevin was the image of a *supportive fellow professional.** Both Rachel and Kevin were perceived and treated not as 'just students' nor as 'teacher's helpers' but as novice professionals. All that a mentor does and says is perceived as a model (effective or otherwise) of professional practice by the student-teacher in his or her role as a novice professional.

Various aspects of professional practice are likely to form part of the discussion between mentor and student-teacher:

> *Subject matter* — Gill chose the topic of *angles* for Rachel to fit in with the Year 7 work. Kevin continued to structure his work around the individualized scheme adopted by the school. It may well be that often the student-teacher is fitting into a departmental policy in which decisions about what mathematics to teach, when and to whom have already been made. However, Rachel, in planning the fine detail of the work, and Kevin, in using investigation as a learning style of mathematics were both able to use their initiative and imagination within this structure and thus develop their skills and strategies.
>
> *Pedagogy* — Gill, in particular, was very supportive in helping Rachel adopt good teaching approaches for the low achieving groups, by getting her to consider how to prepare work for pupils whose reading and powers of concentration may be limited and who often experience difficulty and failure with their mathematics. Such discussion can valuably include:

---

* See, for example HMI (1991, p. 23).

- what prior knowledge is needed in order to tackle a new topic;
- what pupils already know and can do;
- the likely outcomes in terms of pupils' learning;
- implications for future planning.

Discipline — Barbara helped Kevin to work out a radically different approach to an individual in the class. Rachel's initial lack of confidence in preparing mathematics for the mixed ability class could easily have led to a lack of motivation and disruptive behaviour. Getting the subject matter and the approach well-matched to the pupils was a major step towards good relationships within the class.

After discussion of the pros and cons of various methods for teaching a particular topic with the student-teacher, the mentor may well lead by example using a technique with a class in which the student becomes the appraiser. Discussion afterwards centres on 'How could we improve?' and 'Where do we go from here?' Mentors can also warn students of potential pitfalls in the topic as they have firsthand experience of these! In this way a natural professional *partnership* develops. The mentor also needs to be sensitive as to when to 'let go'.* Teachers have to develop their own styles of working in the classroom rather than mimicking another's performance.

It was not the case that Rachel depended entirely on Gill, nor Kevin on Barbara, for support during the teaching practice. Rachel enjoys mathematics and had a surfeit of good ideas for teaching it. Kevin showed skill and sensitivity with pupils most of the time. Each interacted freely with the usual teachers of the classes they taught, seeking and receiving help and advice from them as well. The point that is being made here, is that, in whatever capacity they might be needed, it was Gill who had the responsibility for being there for Rachel, and Barbara for Kevin.

The development of a teacher's own personal style has many aspects. There are the teaching skills of working with individuals, small groups and whole classes of pupils. There are listening and observational skills in seeing how the pupils may be thinking about and constructing their mathematics.[†] Observation of sensitive, imaginative and experienced teachers can be of great value in establishing a variety of good teaching strategies, but students often find the observation and the analysis difficult. There is a complexity of events happening at any moment in any classroom. Mentors can help students focus on different aspects of classroom work (for example, organizing a lesson, encouraging more pupils to contribute to a discussion, managing an individualized scheme when several different pupils need help, clearing up after a practical session etc.) and often provide a sounding board while the student is thinking through which styles and strategies might be most appropriate for them as teachers.

* Chapter 1 looks at 'letting go' in more detail.
† Sue Sanders, in Chapter 3, speaks of a *constructivist* philosophy in learning and teaching mathematics. The use of *constructing* here may be read in this sense.

Listening Friend

> ... students on teaching practice are particularly vulnerable. They are isolated from their peers and so do not have ready recourse to open expression of their feelings. (Hodgkinson, 1992, p. 2)

In cases where there is more than one student-teacher in a school, peer support in the form of 'someone to talk to' may be available. In others there may be a 'kindred spirit', perhaps in the form of a younger member of staff. In the absence of anyone else, it is likely to be the mentor to whom students turn for someone to talk to, someone in whom to confide their fears, their joys and the successes and failures associated with the job of teaching. Hence a *listening friend* (almost a counsellor) is likely to be another facet of the mentor role and one for which the mentor may well feel ill-prepared. It is also easy to forget, in the hectic day-to-day life of the school, that the student is a person with a life outside of the teaching practice! This life may feature other full-time students who are perhaps not as sensitive as they might be to the pressures of their friends' full-time job. Other problems (financial, emotional and accommodation) may add to these pressures and have a habit of coming to a head during school experience.

In addition to the problems associated with the pressures of a student lifestyle, students may become ill themselves or have families who suffer illnesses at some point in the school experience. Sezu, whose mother was dying, was often distressed and felt unable to convey her anxiety to staff in the staffroom. It was suggested by her mentor that she have a long weekend with her mother. This extended break gave the student time away from the school and gave the mentor the opportunity to explain to a caring staff why Sezu was often withdrawn and that she needed support personally as well as professionally.

Mature students may have different concerns. Emily, a single parent with two young school-age children, needed time off from her final teaching practice school in order to look after her injured son. She could not afford extra child-minder fees. The mentor, through close links with the HE Department, was able to put the student in touch with student welfare and financial help was found for her.

In order for the mentor to try to meet the professional, personal and emotional needs of the student, it seems essential that regular times are set aside for meetings with the student, in a setting in which privacy is ensured and confidentiality respected. Availability and approachability seem to be key features in encouraging students to relate to their mentors. One student, Vince, spoke warmly of his mentor who 'made a point of seeing me for a few minutes at the end of every day to ask how the day had gone. It meant that I could get things off my chest before I went home — if I needed to.' Lucy, a mentor, spoke of Liz (a student whose first teaching practice had been with Lucy) coming back to visit her to talk about her new practice and to ask for her advice, since on her subsequent practice she found it hard to talk to her university tutor or to teachers within the school. These examples clear the importance of the relationship which the student and mentor need to develop.

Supportive Critic

The role of *supportive critic* has a certain similarity to the role of *critical friend* used in professional development literature to describe two professionals working together on a common task or problem.* Being a supportive critic involves the mentor observing student-teachers' lessons, offering praise and constructive criticism and supporting them in follow-up activities. The mentor does not necessarily need to have observed the lesson to offer follow-up support, but needs an 'action replay' of the situation on which to focus in order to negotiate the way forward with the student. This action replay may take the form of giving an account of a *critical incident* as described by Stephen Lerman in Chapter 5. The extent to which students are able to describe accurately and to look critically at their own practice is likely to develop with frequent use of critical incidents.

Lucy felt that 'mentoring is easier with the students who come in thinking "I'm here to learn more about teaching" and are open to praise, criticism and support — the ones who can look at themselves'. She considered that an important task for the mentor is 'to assess to what extent the students can evaluate themselves and to what extent you need to do it for them at first while encouraging them to become more self-evaluative'. This is an important judgement for the mentor and possibly one of the more difficult ones as it requires *challenge* as well as support. She said that an aid to this judgment for her was students' differing responses to the suggestion 'What about trying this?' One student's response may be 'Yes, why not?' while another's (possibly implicit) would be 'Why? Isn't what I'm doing good enough?' She felt that at the root of the latter comment was often a set of unrealistically high expectations for the practice coupled with limited skill in making an accurate assessment of one's classroom performance.

Lucy considered that it is important for mentors to remember that the people they are working with are students who are in school 'to learn and grow in the role' and that mentors should try to avoid falling into the trap of expecting more of students than is appropriate at any given time in their professional development. Lucy felt that by making her own expectations of the pupils explicit she could encourage students to be more aware of and more realistic about their own expectations. She felt that observing other maths teachers with differing personalities 'in action' helped as well. Paula, a tutor, relates an anecdote about working in the classroom with a group of student-

---

* See, for example, Day *et al.* (1990). You may like to contrast the more theoretical perspective of *critical friend* offered in Chapter 10 with the practical perspective offered here.

teachers. After the lesson one student commented to her, 'After watching you, I now realize that my expectations for the classroom have been much too high!' Teachers can and should have high expectations for all of their classes but these are hard to achieve and experienced teachers and pupils often fall short. Lucy tried to get novice teachers to be self-critical by always asking them first how *they* thought their lessons had gone. By doing this, her job was made easier in that her main role then was to be a *confidence booster*. She could give praise and offer alternative strategies and support. She preferred to react to the student's reflection rather than be an initiator of criticism which she found tended to build up stress in such a relationship. In addition, she believed that the encouragement of self-evaluative capabilities was essential to a teacher's long-term professional development.*

The role of mentor is likely to be taken in some measure by each member of the mathematics department of a school. Some students' anecdotes describe situations where they felt more criticism than support:

> Some of the teachers came into my lessons and didn't say anything afterwards — just left. When I asked them how they thought it had gone, they said things like 'It was fine'. One of them only watched the last lesson I taught with his class, gave me no feedback whatsoever and yet he wrote 'is not suited to secondary school teaching' on the report he gave to the head of maths. (Sarah, student-teacher)

> I don't like it when people observe you and sit at the back writing all the time. I much prefer it if part-way through they come and talk with you about how things are going, perhaps throw a few ideas around. My friend who's on teaching practice now says that, when they ob-serve her, all the teachers seem do is write about what she's doing wrong. That happened to me as well. Comments like 'You should have told him to take off his coat' were particularly irritating. It's nice to know what you're doing right too! (Nick, in first year of teaching)

Such comments from student-teachers are not uncommon. Lucy stressed the importance of liaising with staff regarding what to look for in classroom observation and what constitutes appropriate feedback. She said, 'There is an assumption that everyone can supervise students although no one has had any training!' Lucy felt that the whole issue of classroom observation needs not only to be sensitively handled but needs to be regarded as an important part of every individual's professional development.

The role of supportive critic, with student-teacher, mentor and tutor col-laborating together, is the source of formative evaluation of the school experi-ence or teaching practice. The summative evaluation may well require the mentor and tutor to adopt a role of both *assessor* and *evaluator*. However the

---

* See Chapter 10 for a development of these ideas.

good relationships developed can enable this to be a positive experience and the student can be involved in the final evaluation and in the writing of any necessary reports. This allows the process to be enabling and affirmative. Chapter 9 explores evaluation in greater depth.

Gatekeeper and Guide

Another important aspect of the mentor's role is that she is both *gatekeeper* and *guide* for the student-teacher with regard to the social setting — the school.* As an insider it may be the mentor who helps the student-teacher initially to 'see' the school and to gain access to its social and mathematical culture. She may provide knowledge about the backgrounds and abilities of the children and what to expect from them. The mentor may explain the system within the school, knowing about discipline, sanctions and rewards and know what is likely to work in mathematics classrooms within the school. It is the mentor to whom the student and tutor would normally first turn to for advice. In some schools the mentor may work closely with a professional tutor and/or deputy head. The latter may well take responsibility for explaining wider school issues and the ethos of the school to students.

To what extent should a mentor be a *welcomer* or *introducer*? How important is it that student-teachers should be introduced to staff outside the department so that they know who staff are and so that staff know them as more than 'just students'? How are novice teachers introduced to those they are to teach? Many student-teachers complain of the indignity of not being introduced to classes when they are 'just observing' claiming that this makes it difficult to establish their status when they take over these classes. Such introductions, made consciously by the mentor and not overlooked in the hurly-burly of school life, help make the situation less threatening for the novice teacher. Lucy often introduces a student-teacher to the class as 'a colleague and friend from — who wants to work with you for — weeks. He will be working with me and you. He will be working with you in small groups initially to get to know you and will then take over the lessons and I will be supporting'. Other mentors will use a variant of this introduction that fits their situation.

HMI indicated the need for a gatekeeper and guide role in the more general induction of students into teaching.

> The central role of teachers in initial training is the supervision and guidance of students in schools. It takes many forms but essentially involves support for the students' *classroom teaching* on the one hand and a variable *involvement in their more general induction into the professional role of teachers on the other.* (HMI, 1991, p. 22; our italics)

* See also Nias *et al.* (1989).

Shaheen, a mentor in an 11–14 high school was, unusually, both in the position of providing support for the students' classroom teaching of mathematics and of providing a more general induction programme — pointing out different ways in which the school met the needs of the pupils. He emphasized the importance (equal to the subject support given by the mathematics department) of the induction programme for students and its value in helping them to be better informed and more sensitive when facing everyday problems, particularly those associated with the role of the form tutor.

Link Agent

Liaison is an important aspect of the role of mentors. They are required to establish and maintain links with a variety of individuals within the school. Other teachers may need to be introduced to the students, their course, and the expectations of the HE Department. Time may also be set aside for students to familiarize themselves with staff and policies from various areas of the school, such as English as a Second Language, Special Needs and Pastoral Departments. The programme also ought to include time for mentors, students and tutors to meet together

For the liaison to work well it seems important that the mentor is conversant with the ideas, beliefs and expectations of HE tutors as well as school staff. Does the mentor have firsthand experience of the educating institution? Has the mentor met the mathematics education staff and seen the facilities available to the students? Much will depend on the extent to which the HE Department involves mentors in planning and teaching mathematics and professional studies courses and interviewing prospective students as well as encouraging them to become involved in such activities as mathematics education seminar programmes. It is equally important for the tutor to know what is going on in the school. Some mentors are able to foster an atmosphere of critical evaluation and challenge alongside the supportive aspects of their work. Others, because of inexperience, lack of time or not being mathematics specialists may not be in a position to do this. Between them, the mentor and tutor ought to ensure all aspects of teacher development are covered, as discussed in more detail in Chapter 2. For a partnership between schools and the HE Department to work well, time needs to be made for mentors and tutors to talk through common aims and issues of concern. In one such partnership, mentors and tutors have two meetings per term, both after school. All agree that some commitment of 'quality time' during school hours would be more beneficial. However the link is structured, the mentor could be encouraged to use the HE Department as a first port of call. Mentors need support too.

Perhaps the most important qualities for a mentor are good interpersonal communication skills and a willingness to work consciously at developing and maintaining productive working relationships with all concerned in the teaching practice experience — even when the going gets tough! Shaheen suggested that a particularly delicate area in which negotiation may be needed and which requires 'tact, diplomacy and sensitivity' is handling pupils either from one's own class or another teacher's whom the student-teacher is currently teaching. Some pupils may resent their 'own teacher' being replaced and may be un-cooperative and 'tell tales' to the usual class teacher. Others are only too delighted at the prospect of a different face. Class teachers may be apprehensive at the prospect of having to re-establish relationships with members of the class once the student has left and may worry that they will have to pick up the pieces. The degree to which these issues become problematic is likely to be related to the manner in which staff perceive student-teachers and the status which they publicly accord them. Much also depends on the ways in which the mentor, student-teacher and class teacher actively work together to anticipate and resolve these issues.

Concluding Remarks

The theme which permeates this chapter is that of *working together*. Both components of the phrase are important. The first stresses that the roles and relationships involved in the mentoring process need to be worked on. They do not necessarily develop in a productive way without the conscious coop-eration of all concerned. The second component reminds us that the school experience is a partnership involving many partners all with differing roles to play. Participants need to be clear about these roles and they need to commun-icate openly and effectively if the teaching practice is to be a successful and rewarding experience for all concerned. At the heart of the whole process is the key figure of the mentor.

References

Day, C., Whittaker, P. and Johnston, D. (1990) *Managing Primary Schools in the 1990s: A Professional Development Approach*, London, Paul Chapman.

Her Majesty's Inspectorate (HMI) (1991) *School-based Initial Teacher Training in England and Wales*, London, HMSO.

Hodgkinson, K. (1992) *A Study of Student Roles and Personal Relationships During Primary School Teaching Practice*, Loughborough, Loughborough University Department of Education, Papers in Education.

Nias, J., Southworth, G. and Yeomans, R. (1989) *Staff Relationships in the Primary School: A Study of Organizational Culture*, London, Cassell.

Southall, C. and King, D.F. (1979) 'Critical incidents in student teaching', *Teacher Educator*, **15**, 2, pp. 34–36.

Chapter 5

Reflective Practice

Stephen Lerman

This chapter develops the idea of reflective mathematics teaching, offering the 'critical incident' as a device to stimulate reflection on teaching. Through examples and case studies and the issues that they raise, it suggests to mentors ways in which student-teachers might be encouraged to develop their own reflective practice.

Introduction

For the mentor, the aim of this chapter is to offer a particularly fruitful way of helping student-teachers to be confronted with mismatches between their expectations of the job of teaching and of the nature of children's learning, and what happens in classrooms, that is, using critical incidents to develop reflective skills. The idea of reflective practice has been mentioned earlier, in Chapter 2, and its meaning will, I hope, become clear through this chapter. I will be taking it to mean developing the skills of sharpening attention to what is going on in the classroom, noticing and recording significant events and 'working' on them in order to learn as much as possible about children's learning and the role of the teacher. In fact, extending beyond the initial teacher education course, I believe that the tools mentors can offer to enable students to learn from what they notice are the same tools that can be used throughout one's teaching to develop and improve. The three-way relationship, between student, tutor and mentor becomes a very rich one here, as mentor and tutor help students to focus on particular, important aspects of the classroom, and then respond to what the students observe, enabling them to generalize their growing awareness and understanding.

Critical Incidents in the Classroom

I will be giving a number of examples through anecdotes here. Now I am not suggesting that *all* anecdotes are useful. Whenever a group of teachers sit around together, we slip into stories of our classrooms and the anecdotes fly around the room! However, for the most part these anecdotes reinforce our opinions, beliefs or prejudices. I am referring here to what are termed *critical incidents*, and by this term I mean ones that can provide insight into classroom learning and the role of the teacher, ones that in fact challenge our opinions and beliefs and our notions of what learning and teaching mathematics are about. Consider the following anecdote:

> A young school pupil does well in number work. When interviewed and asked to talk about her work, she says, 'I know what to do by looking at the examples. If there are two numbers I subtract. If there are lots of numbers I add. If there are just two numbers, and one is smaller than the other it is a hard problem. I divide to see if it comes out even and if it doesn't I multiply.'

There are a number of important points that arise for me from this anecdote and I have listed them below. Before reading my list you might like to record anything which for you is significant in the anecdote.

Internal to the incident:

- good 'performance' is not a certain indication of understanding;
- interviews are often excellent ways of gaining information about children's thinking and, if possible, time could be made available in school for students to be able to carry out some interviews with pupils;
- the 'messages' that children pick up from classroom activities are not necessarily the same as the ones that teachers think they are offering;
- the tasks that children interpret the teacher to be setting (e.g. wanting correct answers in as short a time as possible) may not be what the teacher intends;
- ticking work strongly reinforces behaviour which is seen to lead to success, but the method of reaching the answer may be mathematically incorrect.

Stepping outside the incident:

- anecdotes can be useful in learning about teaching since they allow issues to be raised and discussed.

As far as the role of the mentor is concerned, the last point concerning the use of such anecdotes is the one that I will be focusing upon most in this chapter. I will be suggesting that the following tactics can be part of a most fruitful process for learning about teaching:

- noticing interesting events or critical incidents in the classroom;
- finding ways of recording those incidents, even in the heat of a lesson;

- having the opportunity to reflect on those incidents, with the mentor, colleagues, other teachers, HE tutors and through reading related literature.

At the same time students develop a style of reflecting on their teaching that they can draw upon throughout their careers as teachers.

Before analyzing what this means any further, here is another anecdote to help clarify what critical incidents are:

A young child was asked to count the dots in this picture:

She replied, 'seven'.

When asked to take the teacher through the counting, the child correctly counted up to six, and then pointing to the collection which I have encircled below, said, 'And those three make seven'.

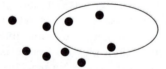

Again, this incident offers a great deal in terms of insight into children's thinking about mathematics, and the role of the teacher. I will attempt to specify below what makes this, for me, a *critical* incident, but first some comments on what might be taking place here, for the child and for the teacher. Many of us might react to the original answer of 'seven' by thinking that the child cannot count. Teachers do not usually leave things at that, though, and this teacher asked the child to explain. The answer showed that the child could count perfectly well but that something else was, in a sense, getting in the way of the right answer. What that something was is anyone's guess! Unfortunately, the teacher did not ask the child what she had been thinking, as there was an interruption at that moment. My own thought was that a parent, or perhaps someone serving lunches, had suggested that three small sweets or potatoes are the 'same' as each of the others, which were larger. Perhaps the arrangement of the three blobs rather resembled the figure '7'. (What's your guess?)

One can imagine the damage to that child's confidence if the teacher had simply said 'Wrong' or had classified the child as a slow learner. In deeper terms, the anecdote illustrates that children bring all kinds of connections and meanings into their cognitive development and teachers need to be aware of that. Again, the general point I am making is that incidents such as these *can* lead to learning about children and about teaching in a far more effective way than any number of lectures. I emphasize 'can' because it has to be said that a necessary element in students learning from these incidents is that they problematize or question the business of teaching and their own learning, and not all students will do that. One of the most important roles of tutor and mentor is to try to make students aware that we all bring entrenched ideas to situations (particularly teaching since we have all been pupils) and one needs to examine and question those ideas if one is to gain from a teacher education course.

Incidents occur in the classroom with great rapidity and teachers have to make on-the-spot decisions in order to deal with those incidents. Critical incidents are those that offer a kind of shock or surprise to the observer or participant. We recognize in them the possibility that further analysis may bring about a shift in understanding about children's learning, the role of the teacher, or the nature of mathematical activity. The criticalness is not, of course, inherent in the experience or event; what is critical for one person may well not be so for another. The two incidents above are critical for me in different ways. Here is a third which was critical for the teacher who recorded it:

> While working around the related areas of proportion and percentage, I gave the class the following question (Year 11, low attainers):
>
> > In a village of 1500 people there are 750 ginger haired people, 450 black and brown haired people and 300 blonde haired people. Describe a typical group of 100 people from the village.
>
> I expected to have to do some discussion work about the meaning of the word *typical*, but I had not expected this: one pupil, Penny, insisted that it depended on who had misbehaved in the village. It took me a few moments of confusion before I suddenly pictured one of Penny's elders, upon seeing her do something naughty, saying, 'That's typical!'.

Noticing and Recording Critical Incidents

One way which I have found fruitful for students to engage with reflection on teaching is to keep a log or journal. If such a log is used as a resource it will probably have been agreed by the mentor and the tutor at the start of the course and will include entries from all parts of the course. The mentor's role would be to encourage the student to use the log in their process of learning from their school experiences, and this is the main focus of the discussion here, although I will also be making remarks about the use of the log in general.

Students should start to use it right from the beginning of their course, and I have found that a good introduction is to get students to write about their own learning experiences in school and in higher education: their images of what learning is all about; the role of the teacher in the light of these experiences and views; and their own aims for education. (You may recall Sue Sanders' focus, in Chapter 3, on 'What is mathematics? What is learning? What is teaching?') They could also be asked to repeat the task at the end of the course, to help them reflect on their learning during the year. This task sets the tone for the whole log, namely reflection, evaluation and, as far as possible, honesty. The last point is obviously connected with the issue of assessment and who might read the journal. The privacy of the log, which allows its fullest use, has to be balanced with assessment demands of the HE Department. A well-kept log will be a rich source of anecdotes for critical analysis.

The log can be used to record all kinds of incidents which the student considers important, including ones that occur in seminars, observations, reading, and their own teaching activities. There is always so much going on, especially in the classroom, that noticing significant events and recording them for later reflection and evaluation are skills that have to be developed. Making a mental note to think about it afterwards is likely to lead to an event being forgotten. It is important that students record events and incidents from the whole range of activities during their course, not just the classroom, because other things can provide important learning experiences too (talking to other adults about their mathematical learning experiences and their feelings about mathematics, for example). Focusing one's attention such that one notices meaningful events is a skill that has to be developed whether it be during one's teaching or at other times. One experienced teacher, for instance, noted an article as being an eye-opener for him, and he set about changing the way he had been teaching for the past twenty years as a consequence. The article described some of the skills Brazilian market children showed in mental computation, skills that they could not demonstrate in their classroom. In Chapter 1 Anne Watson gives other instances of experienced teachers learning from comments and observations from students.

I want to emphasize that the focus of my use of the terms 'noticing', 'important', 'meaningful' and 'critical incidents' is on the student. A mentor or tutor, or teacher for that matter, cannot *provide* meaning for a student, nor a sense of what might be critical. We can and should offer a range of activities, ideas, literature, anecdotes etc. to stimulate noticing and encourage a critical faculty. I have mentioned talking to other adults and also reading articles above. Students can often learn a great deal by looking at prerecorded videos of lessons as a group and with a tutor and/or a mentor if possible, seeing what other people notice, and helping them to sharpen their attention for the classroom.*

---

* This technique is discussed in detail in Mathematical Association (1991).

Yet another example of a different kind of activity that students might be offered comes from some work I did with students on a four-year BEd for teaching in primary schools before they went into their first teaching practice. We had discussed at some length issues of the language of the teacher, children's language, and mathematical language, and the mismatches and multiple meanings that are around in the classroom. During their teaching practice, they carried out a small-scale research task to investigate this. The task concerned how children would respond to a traditional Piagetian test of 'conservation', but with the language changed. In the traditional format children around the age of 7 are shown some blue and brown beads and are asked whether there are more blue beads than beads. In the changed test, based on the assumption that the complexity of the language of the beads is a significant factor, the question concerned daffodils and tulips and whether there were more daffodils than flowers (ATM, 1987). The 'success' of those children using the revised format was increased. One student-teacher recorded the following:

> It really brings home how little I know of how children learn. With later reflection I must agree . . . that the choice of language seems to make a significant difference to a child's response.

As tutor I learnt something from this too, that I should talk less and offer more opportunities for students to work with children on tasks that enable them to notice for themselves. Thus arranging activities described here and in other chapters in this book, such as watching one child at work, interviewing individual children, working with small groups, trying out small research studies, and so on, are valuable ways of helping students notice important things and learn from them.

I have often referred here to mentor and tutor. I do not want to suggest that they have the same function, rather that they are complementary. The role of the mentor, both in general and specifically in relation to the use of the log, is to encourage, highlight, stimulate and guide the student in learning about the learning and teaching of mathematics. The tutor from the HE Department is probably best situated to extend those experiences, across schools and into the literature and to help the student analyze the implications and generalize the outcomes. It would be surprising if there were not some considerable overlap of roles, however, and there should be room for negotiation and especially communication between mentor and tutor regarding the student's learning.

Noticing and recording are the essential first steps to using reflection to learn about teaching. They are not, of course, sufficient. The mentor needs to provide the opportunity and guidance for analysis of what is recorded, enabling a sharpening of noticing.

- Why are those particular incidents significant for the student?
- What appears to be happening? What do others think?

- Can the mentor offer some additional insight?
- What can be found in articles or books that will add information and analysis (the tutor's role perhaps)?

The next section offers some ideas as to how to use those events to encourage students to learn about teaching.

Using Critical Incidents

The extracts below are adapted by Richard, an inexperienced teacher, from his journal and illustrate the way that critical incidents can inform a teacher's understanding about children and about teaching.*

> With one pupil, Claire, I was reviewing a mental arithmetic test in which she had had to calculate one-third of twelve. Claire is in year 11 (aged 15) and working on the SMP 11–16 Graduated Assessment scheme. The level to which she has graduated so far should imply that finding one-third of twelve is within her capabilities. She had given the answer two. She explained how:

> | Claire (C): | Halve it into three. |
> |---|---|
> | Teacher (T): | How? |
> | C: | Half twelve. Six. |
> | T: | Yes. |
> | C: | Then half again. Three. |
> | T: | Yes. |
> | C: | Then half again, two. Oh no, it doesn't work. Can't halve three. |

> After Claire realised that her method would not work to find one-third of twelve, she became very confused in further discussion, seeming to panic, blurting out unreasonable answers, seemingly unable to think straight. It would have been counter-productive to pursue the problem at this stage but I realized that I could not end the interview without causing myself considerable problems in future discussions with Claire. I did not want to have Claire believe that talking to her mathematics teacher could only be an ordeal.

At this stage Richard is aware both that he wants to bring Claire further on in her mathematical understanding and that she has panicked and he must try to help her deal with that. He first deals with the mathematical issue.

---

* Taken and adapted from Lerman and Scott-Hodgetts (1991).

I then gave Claire four two pence pieces and four one penny pieces and proceeded:

> T: How much is that? [Gives money].
> C: 12p.
> T: Here are three people. [Draws three stick figures] Share the money equally between them.
> C: [Places money as shown].

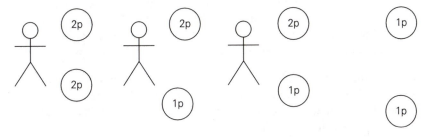

> C: There's two left.
> T: Okay, how much do they each have?
> C: [Pointing correctly] He has 4p, he has 3p and he has 3p.
> T: What about this two pence then? [Points to remaining pennies].
> C: I can't split that, it wouldn't be fair.

Richard has to try and interpret the nature of Claire's mathematical ideas here, in order to decide what activity to offer her next. He takes her answer to imply that Claire has focused on the coins as objects, not on the values of those coins. This emphasizes and reinforces what one notices is happening at the start, namely that children don't just take on board what we 'teach' them; they construct their own knowledge and methods, and also their own interpretations of what we are asking them to do. The teacher then has to try and understand the child's construction in order to take her or him on further.

> T: Okay. Take the money back. Now, your task is to share all the money between the three people so that each person has the same amount in pence and there is no money left over.

> Next lesson, Claire strode in, declaring her success, and showed me the correct solution. What amazed me was not the fact that she had solved the problem, somehow I had never doubted that she would, but that she had the capacity to be such a confident and assertive person. I had never seen this in her before.

Again both aspects of his concern over Claire are apparent, her reactions to success or failure and the development of her mathematical understanding.

Regarding the latter, Richard used Claire's solution as a starting point, explaining that, because there were three equal amounts of money, each pile was one third of twelve pence. He then said the following:

> I was guessing that this was a problem of language because Claire had thought that to find a third of something she had to halve it three times; because she had created an incorrect algorithm to find a third of something; and because her understanding of a third of something was attached to the algorithm she used. I explained to Claire that to find a third of anything, it had to be divided into three equal parts (I was using suitable gesticulations to try to give concrete meaning to my words) and that each part would then be a third of the whole.

On testing her understanding by giving another abstract problem (what is one third of eighteen?) Richard discovered that his explanation had not been enough to dissuade Claire from applying her original algorithm within this context. He then made the following generalization:

> Starting from this point: we have a problem set in a familiar context, with the pupil having a firm grasp of the concepts which form the basis of the problem as stated. We are offering the opportunity for the pupil to develop her thinking. This contrasts with my initial approach with Claire, which entailed me trying to explain to her what a third was. So my reflections led me to this point. I began to believe that if the didactic approach was not good enough for Claire, it was not good enough for any pupil; that instruction and explanation by the teacher had its place in outlining the problem, but not somehow giving mathematical ideas

Concerning Claire's anxiety about mathematics, he again felt that he had learnt something, both specifically about Claire and also more generally about learners.

> On consequent occasions I found that simply giving Claire the option to say, 'I am beginning to panic' meant that the problem could be alleviated . . . Once Claire had a problem which she understood and once I knew that she was solving the problem that I had set, her whole persona changed. Solving the problem with the money might have been the first time Claire has done any mathematics in ages.

Although Richard is a practising teacher and these are reflections on incidents that occurred in his own class, I hope it is clear that a focus on critical incidents can be fruitful for students as well as those with more experience. Obviously the mentor and the tutor will need to respond to whatever particular experiences the student-teachers offer. The critical incidents are *particular* and the mentor, and the tutor especially, can offer the *general* — that is to say other readings, research etc. which may lead to a wider understanding.

Richard's report provides insights at several levels which can serve as examples of how students could be encouraged to investigate further:

- The method Claire uses for finding fractions of amounts is obviously problematic and may be not uncommon. A possible interpretation is that, for Claire, to find a fraction of an amount is to halve, and the '3' in the actual fraction required tells her how many times to do that halving. One can direct the student to look at some of the research literature on fraction work, for example that of Daphne Kerslake (1986).
- Claire's own construction of her mathematical knowledge needs following up, even if only for students to gain an understanding of what goes on for pupils in a classroom. We all construct our own knowledge in learning situations, and clinical interview techniques allow some access for the teacher into the thinking of the child. Mentors can provide opportunities for students to do that (for some developed work on clinical interviewing one could direct them to Steffe, 1991, for example).
- Richard made some generalizations about learning and teaching. In particular he suggests that if his explanations, as a method of transmitting knowledge, are not successful for Claire, perhaps they are not successful for anyone. He says that his experience confirmed what he had read about children constructing their own knowledge rather than receiving it from the teacher. The tutor can direct students to some of the literature on constructivism as a theory of learning, such as the collection of studies of children and classrooms, and also ideas and theories, edited by Ernst von Glasersfeld (1991).*

In this way, theory and research about learning and teaching which the tutor can offer and the practical experiences of the students under the guidance and stimulus of the mentor are integrated. This opportunity for integration is potentially one of the greatest advantages of partnerships in initial teacher education between schools and HE Departments. These bring students into schools for a much greater percentage of their time on the course.

The notion of the mentor's guidance and stimulus is important in another sense too. The students may well need some specific input from the mentor in order to get some sense of what 'noticing' critical incidents might mean. Many students will focus on incidents for themselves, but where this does not happen, the student could, for example, be invited to use a small diagnostic test that might reveal some unexpected mathematical conceptions of the pupils, or a short article that pinpoints a significant issue.† This would be designed to highlight a mismatch between their expectations of children's

---

* Sue Sanders discusses implications of constructivism for teaching in Chapter 3.
† For example, students could refer to the article by Smith (1989) which looks at methods his pupils actually *use* for arithmetic calculations, in contrast to the methods they were taught.

learning, or of the role of the teacher, and what they notice, which is an essential feature of learning through critical incidents.

This brings us to the final section of this chapter, which is a brief elaboration of the origins and meaning of the idea of *reflective practice*.

Some Concluding Thoughts on Reflective Practice

In recent years there has been a reaction against calling our concern in this book 'teacher training'. The word 'training' carries connotations of getting animals to do things as responses to particular stimuli, or to prepare someone to perform mechanical operations on, say, a factory production line, or to run fast. Teaching isn't like that, of course. You may have your lessons well prepared and you may know your class very well indeed, but nevertheless, as I mentioned above, the teacher is constantly faced with events that require an informed decision, usually instantly. One thinks immediately of a potential behaviour problem, such as an abusive comment from one child to another. It could equally be an incorrect answer to a question such as 'If $x + 5 = 12$, what is x?'. The teacher makes some decision as to what to do, based on her or his previous experience, beliefs, prejudices, gut reaction, conjecture about implications of certain decisions and so on. One cannot say that a teacher can be trained to do that!

In the context of engineering, Donald Schön, who developed the notion of the *reflective practitioner*, rejected the distinction between practitioners who could be trained, and theoreticians who did the research, made innovations, and carried out the training. In describing *reflection-in-action*, Schön (1984, p. 5) starts from what he calls the practitioner's *knowledge-in-action*: 'It can be seen as consisting of strategies of action, understanding of phenomena, ways of framing the problematic situations encountered in day-to-day experience.'

When surprises occur, leading to 'uncertainty, uniqueness, value-conflict', the practitioner calls on what Schön terms reflection-in-action, a questioning and criticizing function, leading to on the spot decision-making, which is 'at least in some degree conscious'. Thus Schön is claiming that teachers *are* reflective practitioners, although a degree of consciousness, concerning reflection, is essential*. One sometimes finds, in the education literature, that teachers are being exhorted to *become* reflective practitioners, but this is to misunderstand the point that Schön is making. At the same time that Schön is suggesting that people have too low an expectation of the role of the teacher, and that people should recognize that they draw considerably on experience and on implicit theories and strategies, there are also dangers that one can read too much into reflective practice. By this I mean that one can also find in the educational literature writing under the banner of reflection that appears to be saying very little. In my view, if reflection means looking in a mirror,

---

* See, for example, Scott-Hodgetts and Lerman (1990).

one tends not to see anything new. Even observing is dominated by what one expects to see. This is the essential point; learning from reflection on practice takes place when there is some input, something from outside oneself. To merely record what one does is to learn little.

To summarize the possible activities that can stimulate consciousness of reflection, student-teachers (and teachers) need the input of one or more of the following:

- straightforward observation tasks, with a clear focus, offered by the mentor or by the HE Department;
- small studies or interviews to try out;
- comments and thoughts from observers and participants, especially the mentor, pointing out incidents;
- comments on those incidents from others: mentor, tutors, other teachers, colleagues;
- articles or books whose ideas are discussed, evaluated and criticized.

With these, and equally essential, comes the need for the skills of noticing and of recording, as elaborated in an earlier section.

Finally, I have mentioned research a number of times in this chapter and I want briefly to sketch the links between the ideas elaborated here and research. The aim of all research in mathematics education is the improvement of learning experiences in mathematics and thus the classroom should be seen as the major site of the generation of research issues. Those issues are the direct concerns of the teacher, and while researchers, normally based in universities and colleges, have the opportunity and expertise in research, teachers can and should be integrally involved in studying their classrooms. Much research is *action research*, that is to say research whose focus is to bring about some changes in practice*. An individual teacher might identify a particular problem that she or he feels needs investigation, or a group of teachers might decide to engage with a common problem in a systematic programme of study. They might draw in a researcher for advice and/or collaboration. Clearly some research is more large scale and needs the resources that are sometimes available to people in higher education. The processes upon which teachers will draw in order to identify those issues and develop a programme of research are precisely those which I have described in this chapter. When I have written about the role of the mentor in providing opportunities for students to sharpen their attention, notice incidents, record them and reflect on them, drawing in literature, their mentor, tutors etc. as a way of learning about teaching, the intention is precisely to develop consciousness about the classroom. Whereas the focus for the mentor is to facilitate students' learning about the learning of mathematics, the teacher who has been through this education will be the teacher who can be also an action

---

* See, for example Scott-Hodgetts (1988) and Lerman (1990).

researcher on her or his own practice throughout their career. This is the connection between teacher education and continuing development of teaching that I mentioned at the very start of this chapter and which is taken up again as a major theme in Chapter 10.

References

ASSOCIATION OF TEACHERS OF MATHEMATICS (ATM) (1987) *Teacher as Researcher,* Derby, ATM.

CARRAHER, T. (1988) 'Street mathematics and school mathematics', in *Proceedings of the Twelfth Annual Conference of the International Group for the Psychology of Mathematics Education,* Budapest, Hungary, pp. 1–23.

KERSLAKE, D. (1986) *Fractions: Children's Strategies and Errors,* Windsor, NFER-Nelson.

LERMAN, S. (1990) 'The role of research in the practice of mathematics education', *For the Learning of Mathematics,* **10**, 2, pp. 25–28.

LERMAN S. and SCOTT-HODGETTS, R. (1991) 'Critical incidents in classroom learning — Their role in developing reflective practice', in *Proceedings of the Fifteenth Annual Conference of the International Group for the Psychology of Mathematics Education,* Assisi Italy, Vol. 2, pp. 293–300.

MATHEMATICAL ASSOCIATION (1991) *Develop your Teaching,* Cheltenham, S. Thornes.

SCHÖN, D.A. (1984) 'Educating for reflection-in-action', paper presented at Harvard Business School Anniversary Colloquium on *Teaching by the Case Method.*

SCOTT-HODGETTS, R. (1988) 'Why should teachers be interested in research?' in PIMM, D. (Ed.) *Mathematics, Teachers and Children,* London, Hodder and Stoughton.

SCOTT-HODGETTS, R. and LERMAN S. (1990) 'Psychological/philosophical aspects of mathematical activity: Does theory influence practice?' in *Proceedings of the Fourteenth Annual Conference of the International Group for the Psychology of Mathematics Education,* Oaxtepec, Mexico, Vol. 1, pp. 199–206.

SMITH, R. (1989) 'What's going on in their heads?' *Mathematics in School,* **18**, 5, pp. 33–35.

STEFFE L. (1991) 'The constructivist teaching experiment: Illustrations and implications' in VON GLASERSFELD, E. (Ed.) (1991) *Radical Constructivism in Mathematics Education,* Dordrecht, Kluwer.

VON GLASERSFELD, E. (Ed.) (1991) *Radical Constructivism in Mathematics Education,* Dordrecht, Kluwer.

WALKERDINE, V. (1988) *Mastery of Reason,* London, Routledge.

Chapter 6

Planning for Learning

Pat Perks and Stephanie Prestage

This chapter suggests that planning for teaching implies planning for the learning of pupils, and looks at the role which a mentor might play in supporting a student-teacher's planning. The practicalities of planning and its relationship to the evaluation of teaching are explored through considering the objectives for a lesson.

Introduction

All teachers have to plan for the learning of their pupils. It is probably true that the more experience you have the more idiosyncratic will be the form of your planning. Some aspects of a lesson can be planned beforehand and some develop as reactions to classroom events. For the student-teacher, however, who is learning about the relationship between planning and actual events and who often needs to account to others for their decisions, such planning needs to be overt.

As tutors working with PGCE students we find one of the most rewarding ways of working involves discussion with them of their lesson plans, evaluations and their comments from observing other lessons. The aim of this chapter is to draw attention to aspects of planning — planning for a lesson, planning for observation, the uses of such planning for evaluation — and their role in thinking about teaching and learning. This three-fold nature of planning is shown in Figure 6.1. The context for this discussion will be the lesson plan, its purposes and possibilities, its use as a shared focus between the student-teacher and mentor and as a tool for both the student and the mentor to develop their expertise.

The Purposes of Planning

Planning is essential if a teacher is to offer a coherent range of experiences to pupils. The National Curriculum provides a framework against which pupils

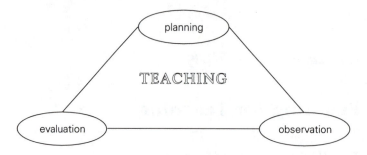

Figure 6.1

will be formally assessed at the end of each of the four key stages, just as the syllabuses for external examinations have done for many years. Such syllabuses, however, do not preclude the necessity of each school having a scheme of work detailing the movement towards fulfilling such requirements.

The mathematics department will have aims for the teaching of mathematics within the school as well as approaches to teaching, content, resources and equal opportunities issues. The department may be using a published scheme to provide material for teachers and pupils.

With all this information why should further planning take place? Long-term aims such as the independence of the pupil as learner can only be achieved through the lesson by lesson experiences offered. The objectives for each lesson will vary in order to offer opportunities to achieve different aspects of long-term aims, to look at different content or even to allow for the different moods of the pupils (is it the first or last lesson of the day, for example). Pupils learn in different ways, so planning needs to ensure that there is provision for a balance of activities and a variety of situations.

Lesson Planning

Students are asked to write lesson plans as explicit statements of their planning. Why should this be so? First of all, it would be foolhardy to go into a lesson unprepared without having thought through the intentions for the lesson. Writing plans makes students articulate what they think will happen. These ideas might be in the form of preliminary sketches or a detailed procedure but, whatever the shape, such a plan will provide the basis for either private or shared reflection on the ways in which the intended lesson develops.

Second, thinking about a lesson plan before the lesson actually takes place can serve a number of purposes. Individual reflection can be important in helping the student to rehearse various aspects of the lesson. Discussion with others can help to refine ideas and prepare for any difficulties that can be foreseen. Shared reflection on a lesson plan can also provide a forum to generate further ideas. In our experience the more students write down at the planning stage the more likely they are to be receptive to the ideas of others and to use those experiences to generate further ideas of their own. Talking allows the asking of questions about the decisions taken and the consequences for classroom practice. Responding to questions such as 'why?' and 'what if . . .?' will help the student discriminate the important aspects of the lesson, reflect upon the particular choices made and thus begin to improve the experiences planned for the pupils. Initially these questions are more likely to be prompted by the mentor, who, in the early stages of the practice, will help to check the decisions that the planner has made about a particular lesson, its balance, the range of experiences and the aims for the pupils.

Third, the lesson plan provides a basis for discussion and evaluation after the lesson, to consider issues such as whether the lesson went according to plan, what changes were made, what did the pupils do, what have they learned and so on. Looking at earlier lesson plans offers a way of examining how thinking has changed and enables the mentor to help a student analyze these changes. The lesson plans provide a history of the student's thinking about lessons and enable the student to trace progress, as in:

- this is where I was;
- this is where I am now;
- why and how have I changed?

Finally, often students and mentors work together in a lesson. Formalizing the organization of the lesson allows negotiation of the roles of these people within the classroom. It is useful to clarify the different roles, especially for the student, who needs to be aware of such things as authority shifts. Possible roles might be:

- the student and mentor sharing the teaching on an equal basis;
- defining a lead person with a helper;
- an observer, with a particular role, looking at preidentified aspects of the lesson.

By planning for these roles, the experienced teacher no longer has to be seen as the authority figure and critic but as an expert helper who, chameleon-like, will take on whatever activity suits the student's need.

Lesson planning in the early stages of teaching is not easy. The experienced teacher can often take it for granted and not see the difficulties which students face. Mentors could take students through the planning process of one of their own lessons. This is often even more valuable if students observe this lesson so that they can begin to recognize the differences between the intended and actual lesson and begin to ask about why such changes occur. Recognition of the difficulties and sharing of the planning process can make the whole issue more active and less threatening so that both student and mentor gain from the insights such planning provokes.

```
┌─────────────────────────────────────────────────────────┐
│  Year 7, Second set.                                     │
│  Objective:    to learn about percentages of quantities  │
│  Equipment:  pupils' books, worksheets                   │
│  Introduction: Explain percentages,                      │
│                Worked example 10% of £35 (5 mins)        │
│                                                          │
│                 10      35                                │
│                ─── x   ──  =                              │
│                100      1                                 │
│                                                          │
│    Worksheet (35 mins)                                   │
│    Read out answers (5 mins)                             │
└─────────────────────────────────────────────────────────┘
```

Figure 6.2

The Planning Process

Styles of Planning

A lesson plan is intended to be a helpful record which describes the thinking about the lesson before the lesson itself takes place. It can take many forms. There is no one correct way for people to capture their thinking about such a dynamic event. It is for the student and mentor to negotiate the style of the presentation of these ideas so that they come to share a perception of the purpose of these plans and the ways in which they are recorded.

The style of lesson and the amount of detail students include depends upon their individual perceptions of the task. Some need the security of every detail being worked out, a script for each explanation, each answer calculated, every step of a problem worked through. Others only need to record the highlights of the lesson, the drawing that needs to go on the board, the important questions. Some students are unaware of what they need to record, or plan for and may produce a lesson plan which gives no indication of the underlying thoughts or images. Figure 6.2 shows a lesson plan which offers a structure but which gives little indication of whether the student has really thought about the way the lesson might proceed.

The mentor could probe gently to discover what level of preparation has taken place. For example, it may be possible to consider the particular worked example, how questions can differ in style, whether the use of a standard algorithm is necessarily the best way of doing this particular calculation, the consequences of using a standard algorithm, the ways in which ideas can be explained or discovered and what misunderstandings may arise. The mentor might point out that explaining ideas to pupils needs careful consideration. Writing 'explain percentages' gives no indication of how the explanation will be offered or how much the pupils will be involved in the explanation. The mentor could helpfully challenge the student so that her or his image of 'explaining' becomes explicit and the underlying ideas become more readily available to the student. Students often fail to realize the assumptions they are

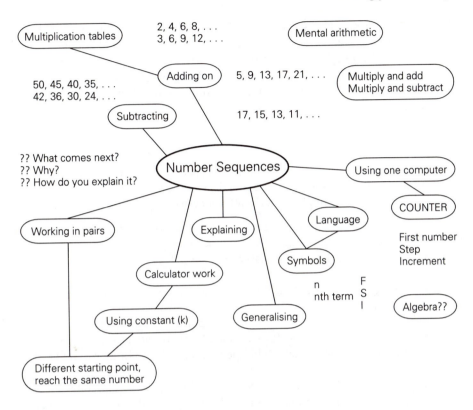

Figure 6.3

making about explaining or about children's prior knowledge or both. Planning can help to expose these assumptions and look at ways they might affect pupils' learning.

One useful planning tool is brainstorming followed by organizing ideas into a web diagram.* Figure 6.3 shows an example of a web diagram based around number sequences. The lack of linearity encourages the jotting down of ideas and indicates the breadth of choices the subject may offer.

As the figure shows, planning in this way may end in a collection of more ideas for work than can be comfortably used in one lesson. But such brainstorming may offer a variety of ideas for starting points, providing the teacher with plenty of choices for a particular lesson, or for several weeks. For example, the possibility of using one computer and a particular piece of software (shown on the figure as the program COUNTER)† may provide the focus of a

---

* Another planning network is offered in the *Preparing to Teach* framework of the Open University's Mathematical *Update* series, published by the Open University (1989).
† COUNTER is a computer program with considerable potential for interesting number work in the classroom. It shows one or two counters which can be controlled by the input of start, step, and increment numbers. It is from Slimwam 1, published by the Association of Teachers of Mathematics.

whole lesson or may be used for five minutes' introductory classwork to allow discussion of the arithmetic operations involved and to provide an element of challenge to the pupils. The shared job for the mentor and student is to explore the possibilities, identify the choices for a particular lesson and then to make decisions about the order of events, timings, questions etc. which may be superimposed onto the diagram.

Content

Whatever form lesson planning takes, it is useful to include details of the orchestration of the lesson, from the practical to a rationale of the mathematics being presented. This might include reference to:

- an equipment list, in order to arrive with everything;
- the order in which the lesson will happen;
- timing of the lesson so that you have a feel for when things might happen;
- some thought about the types of questions to be asked — open/ closed;
- decision-making to be done by the pupils;
- issues about control — for example, If I want them to work in groups, how am I going to make it happen? Am I going to organize the groups or are the pupils?
- pupils: which ones do I need to see? Any areas of difficulty? Praise?
- why should the pupils want to do this? Does this need to be made explicit?
- homework: dealing with what was set previously and subsequent work;
- links with the previous lesson, transitions to the next;
- some thoughts on the use of computers, calculators and graphical calculators.

The practical details of a lesson are often the easiest for students to identify in the initial stages, indicating their concerns in simply surviving. Peter Gates discusses this focus in teacher development in Chapter 2. The issues for learning are less easy to identify and indeed are often not seen as problematic by students. For example, do the students recognize the assumptions in 'explain percentages', as described earlier? The objectives for learning are often expressed in vague and general terms, for example, 'to learn about percentages'. The real heart of the lesson is not fully explored.

Objectives for Planning

Every lesson needs a base on which to plan. Objectives can provide this. Here we are using the word objectives to represent what ought to be achievable for both pupils and students within the lesson. Objectives could be about working in certain ways, learning certain facts or working on a particular piece of

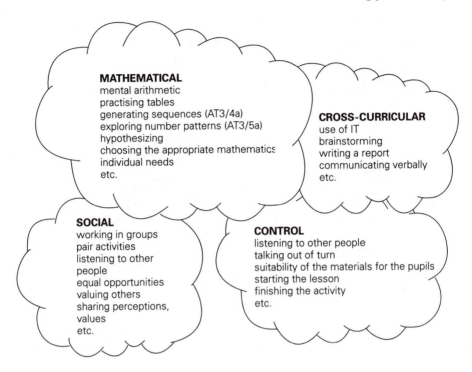

MATHEMATICAL
mental arithmetic
practising tables
generating sequences (AT3/4a)
exploring number patterns (AT3/5a)
hypothesizing
choosing the appropriate mathematics
individual needs
etc.

CROSS-CURRICULAR
use of IT
brainstorming
writing a report
communicating verbally
etc.

SOCIAL
working in groups
pair activities
listening to other
people
equal opportunities
valuing others
sharing perceptions,
values
etc.

CONTROL
listening to other people
talking out of turn
suitability of the materials for the pupils
starting the lesson
finishing the activity
etc.

Figure 6.4

mathematics. It is these objectives which will then form the major reference points for an evaluation and possibly for observation. Such objectives may apply to the whole class or to small groups or even concern an individual.

Every lesson should have been thought about in relation to one or more of the following concerns, which have been grouped for convenience in four areas — mathematical, social, cross-curricular and control. (See the next section for a note about control.) The four headings in Figure 6.4 are ones we have found useful when talking with students. Others may find it more convenient to group such items in a different way. These lists under each of the headings are not exhaustive and it might be a useful exercise for student and mentor to add to them by identifying other concerns that may need to be addressed during a lesson. The lists provide a way of looking at the choices which might be made when designing a lesson. The items are not themselves objectives but can contribute to the formulation of objectives which will of course vary according the needs of the class, the weather, the development of the mathematics, etc.

Examples of pupils' objectives might be:

- to work on the concept of gradient using a graph plotter;
- to produce a written report;
- to explore number sequences.

Find out the size of each jump and fill in the missing numbers in your book

Exercise 1.
1. 2, 4, 6, 8, __, __   2. 3, 5, 7, 9, __, __
3. 7, 9, 11, 13, __, __   4. 11, 13, 15, 17, __, __
5. 0, 3, 6, 9, __, __   6. 1, 4, 7, 10, __, __
7. 2, 5, 8, 11, __, __   8. 6, 11, 16, 21, __, __
9. 25, 50, 75, __, __   10. 30, 50, 70, 90, __, __

Exercise 2.
1. 10, 8, 6, __, __   2. 18, 15, 12, 9, __, __
3. 22, 20, 18, 16, __, __   4. 13, 11, 9, 7, __, __
5. 24, 20, 16, 12, __, __   6. 17, 14, 11, 8, __, __
7. 25, 20, 15, 10, __, __   8. 100, 80, 60, __, __
9. 500, 400, 300, __, __   10. 250, 200, 150, __, __

Figure 6.5

These particular objectives are written in terms of what the pupils will be doing during the lesson. Teacher objectives might be:

- to introduce the class to a graph plotter;
- to enable someone to produce a written report;
- to give every pupil a chance to explore number sequences.

As the mentor and student discuss and define objectives for a lesson it is often helpful to distinguish between teacher objectives and pupil objectives in order to focus on what pupils will be doing and what the teacher will be doing. Such distinctions will also contribute after the lesson to the evaluation of pupils' learning and of teachers' teaching. Likely interconnections between objectives can be seen in Figures 6.6 and 6.7.

Sometimes students are offered very particular instructions on what they are to teach in their lessons by the usual class teacher. These are often interpreted as being precise details about what they have to do and how they have to do it, rather than a prompt on which to build a lesson by analysing possible objectives underlying the ways in which the content may be handled.

For example, suppose a student is asked to use some exercises from the text book for a lesson (Figure 6.5). The student may identify the mathematical objective of the lesson as 'pupils working on recognizing number patterns' without even being aware that the use of exercises in this form implies a particular lesson style, or even questioning whether they could do a different lesson based on this exercise.

The role of the mentor then is to help the student to extract the essence of what they have been asked to teach and to help them make the lesson their own. The dialogue between mentor and student can often prompt many different ideas about how a lesson might develop. Planning together can draw on the different experiences both bring to the discussion. The expertise of the mentor may bring more suggestions, but the need to encourage the student to 'take risks' with different lesson styles may also encourage the mentor to experiment.

Teaching a lesson together can allow the student to get involved in alternative classroom approaches, with the mentor's support, and widen the range of lesson styles available to both. Having worked together, later reflection can focus on issues of joint concern arising from the shared experience.

One strategy that we have found useful is to identify different objectives and then consider how the lesson could change in response to trying to fulfil these objectives. Figure 6.6 takes as its starting point a similar mathematical objective to the exercise illustrated in Figure 6.5 on number sequences. As the figure shows, different lesson ideas have been constructed in response to the prompts provided by other objectives. It also shows how lessons can be designed to explore similar mathematical content while offering different experiences to pupils. A particular piece of mathematical content does not have to be the starting point for this type of exercise. Figure 6.7 offers a mathematical process as a starting point and describes some possibilities for classroom action.

Diagrams such as these demonstrate how lessons can vary according to the objectives chosen. Working with these ideas also enhances the thinking about the choices offered to teachers and pupils. Students often appear to be seeking the one correct way of teaching some material, whereas experienced teachers are aware of the many different approaches needed and possible. The experienced teacher is flexible in both planning and teaching, being prepared to respond to the many signals within the classroom. Planning for flexibility is difficult for students, they often consider that underplanning enables this, whereas in most cases it requires more planning. Thinking about the possibilities shown in Figures 6.6 and 6.7 provides a means of identifying the different ways in which a lesson may progress and introduces versatility and flexibility into the planning process.

A Note About Control

The use of *Control* as a heading for a list of objectives can be contentious as the word has so many perjorative overtones. Yet those classes which have the most freedom often are the most controlled. In order to offer the learner independence while allowing equality of opportunity for all, the teacher has

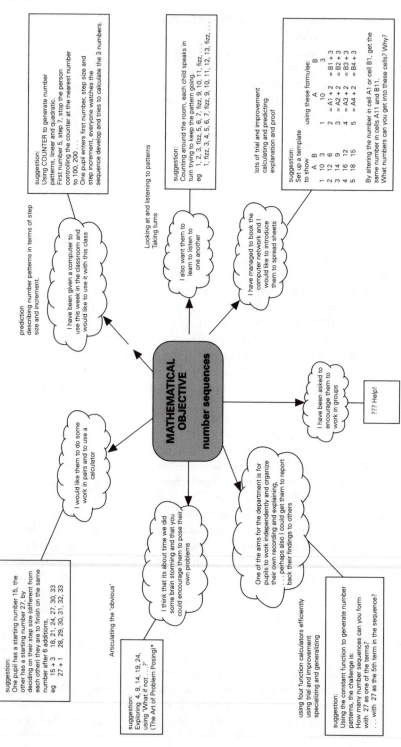

Figure 6.6

* Brown and Walter (1984) The Art of Problem Posing. Philadelphia, Franklin Press.

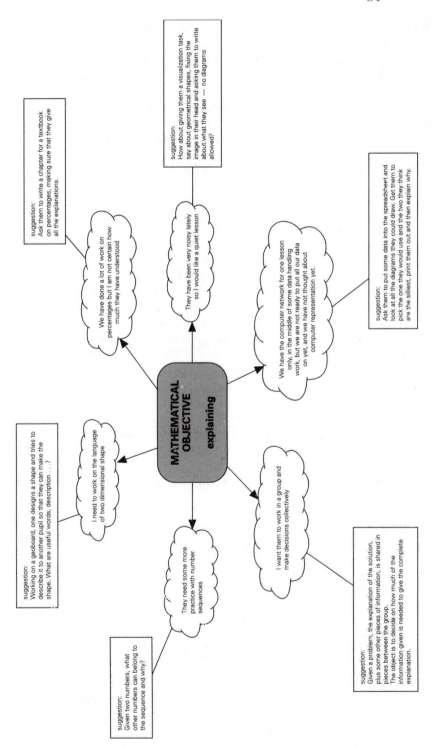

suggestion:
Ask them to write a chapter for a textbook on percentages, making sure that they give all the explanations.

suggestion:
How about giving them a visualization task, say about geometrical shapes, fixing the image in their head and asking them to write about what they see — no diagrams allowed?

suggestion:
Ask them to put some data into the spreadsheet and look at all the diagrams they could draw. Get them to pick the one they would use and the two they think are the silliest, print them out and then explain why.

We have done a lot of work on percentages but I am not certain how much they have understood

They have been very noisy lately so I would like a quiet lesson

We have the computer network for one lesson only, in the middle of some data handling work, but we are not ready to put all our data on yet, and we have not thought about computer representation yet.

MATHEMATICAL OBJECTIVE
explaining

I need to work on the language of two dimensional shape

They need some more practice with number sequences

I want them to work in a group and make decisions collectively

suggestion:
Working on a geoboard, one designs a shape and tries to describe it to another pupil so that they can make the shape. What are useful words, description . . . ?

suggestion:
Given two numbers, what other numbers can belong to the sequence and why?

suggestion:
Given a problem, the explanation of the solution, plus some other pieces of information, is shared in pieces between the group.
The object is to decide on how much of the information given is needed to give the complete explanation.

Figure 6.7

75

to impose structure onto the classroom in terms of behaviour. For many students the issue of control is their major preoccupation when they begin to teach. Their first evaluations are of the form 'They didn't behave themselves', 'I couldn't keep them quiet' etc. The reasons for such poor discipline have many causes, such as the behaviour of the student or the non-cooperation of the pupils, but more often poor discipline and control are a result of poor planning and unsuitable mathematics. The objectives could be couched in terms of classroom management and organization, but as 'control' and 'discipline' are what students talk about, it is perhaps better to use such terms in order to analyze the best way of improving the learning environment for our pupils.

Planning for Observation

One of the most potentially useful aspects of the time spent in school by students is the time they spend in observation. For both mentors and students, working with each other provides one of the few opportunities for both to observe teaching and to observe pupils' activity and learning. Observation of lessons, of students by mentors or of mentors by students, is a process which needs to be planned for as importantly as the lesson itself. The mentor needs to help the student recognize the active role of observation. Students are not always aware of what to look for, their comments about what they have seen can sound negative and unfriendly or vague. To the student, the mentor can often seem overcritical. Building a trusting relationship between student and mentor is crucial. Planning for observation can create an atmosphere where the notion of critical friend can develop.* Part of the planning time needs to be devoted to planning for observation in order that this process can be useful and of benefit to both.

In the initial stages students may need to be helped to focus on particular aspects of the lesson, for example:

- the start;
- the finish;
- board work;
- particular pupils;
- body language;
- the questions pupils ask;
- the questions teachers ask;
- what mathematics the pupils are actually doing;
- what the teacher does when not 'up front'.

By being asked to focus on a particular point students may come to realize what they are looking at and what they are looking for. For example, if students

* Chapters 1, 4, and 10 all discuss the role of a critical friend.

observe the start of lessons in different subjects this may help them to come to an understanding of how they might start lessons, what choices are available and how these choices might affect the pupils' learning.

The mentor will probably try to focus on as many points as possible when watching a student's lesson but it is helpful in the initial stages for the student to be aware of what the mentor is looking at in particular. This particular focus may arise from discussion of the lesson plan, for example, if the student has decided to do some group work with the pupils, the mentor may decide to pick up on observation relating to the groups, how to set them up, how the task affected the ways in which the pupils worked. Eventually such shared experiences may allow mentor and student to negotiate the major points for observation, so that they have a shared basis for further discussion.

One aspect may deal with particular behaviour by the teacher. Some behaviours may be relatively easy to change:

> I remember one of my pupils saying 'Excuse me Miss, but what is your *wont?*' It was only then I realized that I use the phrase 'as is my wont' as a punctuation mark. With the aid of the remark and the diligence of the fourth form, this habit disappeared.

Others need more directed work:

> I was convinced I was fair to the girls in the class, that I responded to them as much as the boys. When someone observed me and did a simple count, I found I had responded to the boys about twice as often. With the help of the observer that began to improve, but I wonder if my behaviour has changed much.

The process of observation is important; students need to be helped to become aware of what happens in their own classrooms by looking at other classrooms. The development of observational skills within students is essential if they are to be aware of the needs of the learners who will be in their care and if they are to notice the influence that they themselves have on their pupils. Many students start by being able to attend to one thing at a time but need to develop a multiple awareness of what is happening in the classroom. Their own skills as teachers can be improved by noticing what other teachers do and using these ideas to improve their own practice.

The observations made by the mentor may either highlight points of which the student was not aware or indeed may provide a different interpretation of what they have both seen. The former may raise new issues for students to consider and perhaps look for in future lessons. The latter provides valuable discussion and it is in resolving different interpretations that the reflective practitioner may develop.*

* The notion of the reflective practitioner is discussed in Chapters 5 and 10.

Lesson Evaluation

In this section the word evaluation is used to describe the process which happens after the lesson has taken place. A written evaluation offers material which may provide important prompts to aid reflection. Evaluation can provide an opportunity for students to record their feelings, what they have noticed, their questions. The evaluation of any lesson is the time when you try to capture your own perception of what happened, matching the lesson outcomes against the chosen objectives to see whether these have been achieved or were achievable. It could be described as planning with hindsight when various questions are considered.

- What did I set out to do and what actually happened?
- What would I do differently if I were to teach this lesson again?
- What went really well and why? How can I build on this?
- Where did the lesson falter? How might a small change have avoided this?
- What were the outcomes for the pupils? How did they match against my objectives?
- What did they learn? How can I tell?
- How well did I respond to the pupils' needs?
- Was I a good listener?
- Where did I get to? Where did the pupils get to?
- Where do I, and they, need to go next?
- Where does the planning for the next lesson begin etc.?

This questioning process offers a vehicle for improving planning and teaching. The experienced teacher can see and handle many things in the classroom and could probably answer all of these questions and more. An inexperienced teacher only has a limited viewpoint, is involved in the moment, concentrates on her or his part and does not see all that is happening. One role of the mentor is to help the student focus on which are the important questions for a particular lesson. For example, the lesson may have been planned using some aspect of Figure 6.6, so the evaluation may raise questions about a particular facet such as reporting back (Figure 6.8) and the related layers of evaluation concerning self, the pupils and the lesson.

Diagrams such as Figure 6.8 may help to identify issues on which the student would wish to work further. This in turn may help to identify different objectives for future lessons. Students will have their scheme of work identifying roughly what their lesson will contain but the evaluation of a lesson should inform the next lesson and help the student to construct the detail of how the next lesson might progress.

As well as working on a particular aspect, the mentor can also help the student identify the important moments of the lesson (good or bad), for example:

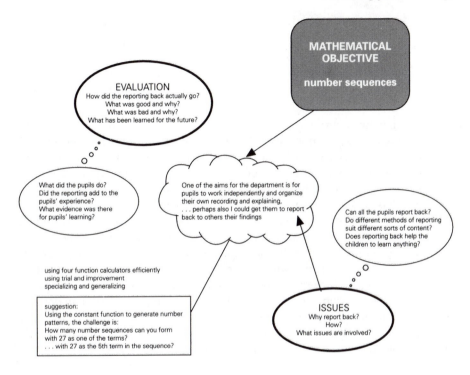

Figure 6.8

- what were the 'golden moments'?
- when did a lesson begin to fail and why?
- where are the 'critical incidents' (as described in Chapter 5)?

Some students are good at analyzing what happens in a lesson but are often overcritical and need help to recognize their good points and how they are improving. Other students need to be helped to develop their critical faculties so they will come to recognize such things as when an explanation served no good purpose or when pupils fail to respond and why.

Evaluation also provides an opportunity to explore the many ways in which things might have been organized differently or what might have been more appropriate for this particular lesson. For example, this might involve helping a student to recognize:

- that getting pupils to work in groups does not happen automatically. How could the activity have been altered slightly to improve the management of group work?
- that if a control objective is to get the pupils not to speak out of turn then perhaps the whole lesson might focus on this and be organized as a chaired debate;

- that brainstorming ideas for a particular task might work without detailed preplanning but for an inexperienced group this needs to be managed carefully;
- that the mathematics within a page of text might need to be made more explicit to the pupils and connections made to previous lessons.

It is difficult for students to recognize everything and they need help to recognize what they do not know. The use of a written report by the student and/or mentor of what has been observed within the classroom acts as an *aide-mémoire* for the questioning process and reflects the individual's perception of what went on. Each can have a different perception of what happened and time has to be spent reconciling the different viewpoints. The way in which this is handled is a vital aspect of the two-way process between student and mentor. The mentor may wish to encourage the student to write a brief but vivid account of the significant moments, rather than a rambling description of the whole lesson and will often wish to write on a student's evaluation as ideas emerge. This ought to be a two-way process. The mentor's written observation of a lesson can be seen to be a negatively critical document and the student must feel able to respond in writing to the comments made. The atmosphere of trust and sharing is one which becomes vital at this vulnerable time for the student.

Working Together

Planning, observation and evaluation are important aspects for the development of the student-teacher and for the growth of the mentor's own skills. Many of these are mentioned throughout this book. How the student and mentor deal with their responsibilities in each of these activities, and in the interaction between the three, needs to be thought through. A shifting balance is required as the student becomes experienced. The existence of a structure against which to consider actions and decisions can help this balance. Students also need support to recognize that they cannot always be successful, and that learning cannot be assumed simply because a class is racing through an exercise.

One important aspect of the work of mentors is to articulate their *own* practice in order to:

- ask the questions to enable the student to realize that there are many questions that might be asked about any one lesson;
- extend the range of teacher choices that can be made about any lesson;
- discover with the student the choices that might be made, making the choices and then planning for the things to happen.

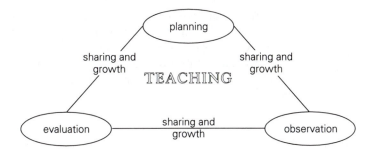

Figure 6.9

Students need to recognize that there are many challenges in learning to teach. Articulating and discussing their planning can help them to recognize the many strands such as learning to adapt to pupils' needs and working flexibly within the classroom.

Teaching is a complex and exciting job. When learning about teaching, it becomes clear that the more issues and questions that are identified the more issues and questions there are to be raised. Encouraging students to articulate their intentions through lesson plans enables the teaching process to be seen to be developing as a result of reflection upon planned action.

Conclusion

This chapter offers what we believe to be a very important triad of actions in planning for learning — planning, observing and evaluating. The interaction between these activities enables the mentor and student to focus closely on the teaching and learning process and offers opportunities for sharing and growth.

Initially, planning for learning is about planning a lesson in order to survive in that lesson. The student-teacher only perceives the role of teacher in terms of *self* and lessons are described in terms of what the student will do. Observation and evaluation help students to recognize the role of pupils in lessons and the effects different actions might have on pupils' learning. As planning becomes more flexible, actions begin to reflect the needs of the class and teaching starts to become a cooperative process between the learners — both students and pupils.

This chapter is entitled 'Planning for Learning' and the reader may be concerned that all that has been discussed is planning for teaching. The planning for teaching is part of the essential learning process for student and mentor. For our pupils, we share a belief with John Mason that: 'Teaching takes place in time, learning takes place over time.'* As teachers, at any particular

* Inaugural address as Professor of Mathematics Education at the Open University (1991).

moment, we can only plan for our own teaching, the learning process is the responsibility of the pupils. By planning our teaching in time to offer a wide variety of experiences and contexts and to meet the various social, control and cross-curricular objectives, we may be able to plan for the mathematical learning of our pupils in the best way possible. By planning for teaching we hope we are planning for learning.

Chapter 7

Interpreting the Mathematics Curriculum

Doug French

This chapter focuses on the mathematics curriculum to consider the mathematics that children learn and how a mentor can help student-teachers become more aware of the way in which their actions contribute to children's mathematical education. Through particular examples of classroom activities it raises issues for the mentor and offers practical suggestions of questions to address with student-teachers.

Introduction

Student-teachers are faced with many conflicting demands and pressures in relation to how they should interpret the mathematical curriculum and the ways in which they should approach teaching mathematics to children. They rapidly discover that teachers, often in the same school, interpret their roles in very different ways and that very different views both of mathematics and how it is learnt are commonly held. They find that their tutors at college or university also have a variety of views and that they may be encouraged by them to question some current school practices. In addition they are aware of the demands for 'good results', particularly in mathematics as a core subject, made on schools by parents, employers and politicians.

Students' own preconceptions about the nature of the task that faces them and how best to go about it are likely therefore to be challenged in many ways. As Sue Sanders pointed out in Chapter 3, they have to come to terms in some way with this variety of views, develop their own philosophy and try to put it into practice. The mentor's role is to help students find their own path by drawing out various key issues, making them aware that there are choices to be made, presenting a range of alternatives and encouraging students to create and use opportunities. In Chapter 4, Rita Nolder, Stephanie Smith and

Jean Melrose explored roles and relationships between mentor and student-teacher and in Chapter 6, Pat Perks and Stephanie Prestage analyzed the processes involved in planning and evaluating lessons. This chapter builds on these ideas to consider the *mathematics* that children learn and how the mentor can help student teachers become more aware of the way in which their actions contribute to children's mathematical education.

Mentoring has to take place in the context of a particular school, where the mathematics department will have its own philosophy which is put into practice through the schemes of work it has developed and the resources that are available. The mentor has the advantage of frequent contact with the student and can use opportunities as they arise to help students develop their own views through bringing together and reflecting on a wide range of experiences within the school. However, student-teachers' experiences in that school, while being a significant part of their course, may not be the only experience they have of working in a school, nor will it be the only context in which curricular issues are discussed. The course tutor has a role in encouraging students to gain a broad perspective of curricular issues and to place their experiences of them in a wider context beyond the school.

To discuss these issues, this chapter considers some matters arising in four differing contexts. The first is a lesson which a mentor observed and the range of issues that arose from this brief seventy-minute 'snapshot' of a student's experience in the classroom. The second is a discussion of a particular curriculum topic: sines and cosines. The third considers the theme of mental calculation that can valuably pervade much classroom activity in mathematics and, finally, an example is given involving the use of a microcomputer in learning mathematics.

A Lesson Observed

Student-teachers rightly expect and deserve some feedback when a lesson has been observed. In providing comment the mentor needs to balance praise and criticism, to encourage the student to reflect on different aspects of the lesson and to suggest areas that particularly need to be worked on. In this chapter the concern is with curricular issues — on what is being taught and learnt — so while the discussion here will focus on these that does not mean other matters are of lesser importance or should be ignored. For example, students are concerned with problems of class control and the behaviour of particular individuals as considered in Chapters 4 and 6 and these are often, although not always, related to aspects of the curricular aims of a lesson.

There are always a multitude of actions and observations arising from any lesson that could be discussed at length. Chapter 5 has shown the value of time spent discussing critical incidents which arise in any lesson. Likewise a discussion concerning alternative approaches to a particular topic or difficulty can be of great benefit. Several such matters are considered here arising from

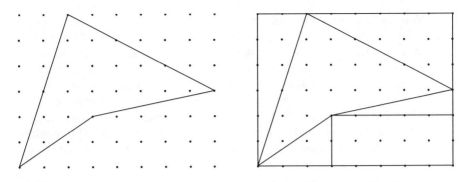

Figure 7.1   Figure 7.2

a lesson, observed by a mentor, with a Year 8 mixed ability class taken by Pat, a student-teacher.

The class was working on the topic of area using booklets from the SMP 11–16 scheme published by Cambridge University Press. They were accustomed to using the booklets individually, but the school had grouped them into 'modules' so that all the children in a class were working on the same general topic at the same time. This made it possible for the teacher to work with the class as a whole from time to time to discuss a new idea or to draw threads together. Pat started the lesson by asking the class to consider the area of a quadrilateral drawn on dotted paper, as shown in Figure 7.1. This was shown on the over-head projector screen and suggestions were invited from the class.

Two ideas were put forward by individuals: one suggested splitting the shape up into simpler shapes and the other suggested putting a 'box' round it. Pat adopted the second suggestion, having prepared a 'box' on another transparency beforehand; this is shown in Figure 7.2. She continued by dividing the outer part of the diagram into a rectangle and four triangles, as shown, and then by questioning the class elicited their areas and, hence, the area of the quadrilateral. This part of the lesson proceeded at a rapid pace, lasting about ten minutes, and then the remainder of the time was devoted to individual work using booklets.

The relationship between Pat and the class was excellent; they were very attentive, contributed constructively to the first part of the lesson and worked conscientiously on their individual booklets in the latter part. Pat had planned the lesson thoroughly and work proceeded in a calm and productive atmosphere. It could fairly be described as a 'good' lesson, and the mentor complimented Pat on its success at the end. Nonetheless there were plenty of matters arising that could be discussed fruitfully.

The mentor began discussion by asking Pat what had seemed significant in the lesson for her. Pat felt that she had dismissed the suggestion that the shape should be split up into simpler shapes rather rapidly with a comment like 'You could do that, but there is a better way', which led another pupil to make the suggestion she wanted. Focusing on this critical incident, as discussed in Chapter 5, the mentor asked her to talk through some alternative possibilities, perhaps to put herself in the place of the boy who had made the first suggestion and think how he might have reacted. Pat suggested that his idea should have been followed up so that the difficulties which would arise could become evident, but that she would then wish to point out that his method could have worked well with a different quadrilateral. The incident provided a way of opening up discussion about several more general issues:

- How do you ensure that a child does not feel 'put down' when they make an unanticipated suggestion?
- How should you react to a 'wrong' answer?
- How do you make children feel that their suggestions are valued?

Another matter, this time raised by the mentor, concerned the extent to which all the class were following what was being presented. The only feedback was coming from those who volunteered suggestions and answers. Again a question served to stimulate discussion:

- How do you know whether children who have not contributed orally have understood the ideas being considered?
- How can you obtain more information about a wider range of children?
- How can you ensure that more children take an active part in some way in a class-led discussion?

Towards the end of the discussion Pat said that she had to set the class homework on the topic of *area*, the next lesson, and that she wondered what would be suitable for a class with a wide range of ability. She wanted something with which they could all succeed, but which was not too trivial for the abler children. This gave the mentor the opportunity to suggest using a task which provided the children with a choice, so that they could respond at their own level, perhaps by asking them to make up some shapes of their own. Pat decided to give them some 'spotty' paper and ask them to produce a number of shapes with an area of $12cm^2$, encouraging them to be as imaginative as possible by suggesting a few interesting possibilities as a starter, as shown in Figure 7.3.

As this account illustrates, a single lesson can provide a wealth of material for discussion and the mentor may find it difficult to decide which of many issues to address. It will often be sensible to look at one or two matters in some depth rather than to cover a wide range superficially. It is also important that mentor and student *agree* on their focus. This might be done in advance of the lesson, for example agreeing to look at styles of questioning and their effect, or at effectiveness of transitions between activities.

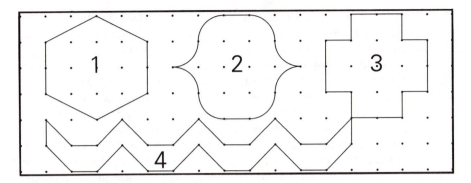

Figure 7.3: Areas of 12 cm²

The mentor's role is to help the student-teacher to develop a critical awareness of the many interrelated issues that arise within a lesson and how these contribute to or detract from each individual child's learning of mathematics. It is very easy to observe a lesson and then to concentrate only on points of criticism in the follow-up discussion. By seeking the student's own perceptions of the lesson first, the mentor can often find non-threatening ways to address issues. As with the boy in the lesson whose suggestion was dismissed, it is wise for the mentor to be alert to how the student-teacher might react to remarks that are made.

Students have to be encouraged to ask their own questions about events, both with regard to their responses to the class and to individual children and in relation to the mathematical activities of the lesson. The mentor can encourage this more often by asking questions than by attempting to give answers. Such questions can enable students to perceive a wider range of choices in planning activities and responding to pupils.

A Curriculum Topic

The student-teacher will certainly expect the mentor to be a source of advice and ideas when it comes to planning how to teach a new topic.* The mathematics department's scheme of work should offer some appropriate ideas to the student, but an enthusiastic student will be keen to try out alternative approaches and should be encouraged to do so. Some students will not be so keen to try the unfamiliar and will prefer to follow what they see as a safe path by always attempting to teach in the way they were taught, rather than considering a choice of approaches. Other students will simply be unaware that alternative approaches exist. The mentor needs to challenge the student to

---

* The Open University Mathematics *Update* series provides a helpful framework for preparing to teach a topic. See, for example, Open University (1988).

think again by occasionally suggesting alternatives, encouraging their use and evaluation in the classroom, and by providing opportunities for observing and working in classrooms where interesting work is going on.

As an example consider an introduction to the sine and cosine functions for a class in year 10. Level 8 of Attainment Target 4 of the National Curriculum requires students to: 'Use sine, cosine and tangent in right-angled triangles'. In planning a sequence of lessons on this theme students need to be clear what they are seeking to achieve; what should pupils understand about sine, cosine and tangent and in what ways should they be able to use them? Students are often overoptimistic in their assumptions about children's prior knowledge and fail to recognize the pace at which they can take in new ideas and learn new skills. Consequently they tend to present too many new ideas too rapidly. It is important to be clear about a minimum knowledge to aim at for all pupils, but also to have ideas about useful and interesting extensions for those who work faster. Providing opportunities to investigate, or to work within a relevant context, can help develop pupils' awareness of the concepts involved.

For example, a pupil, looking at a scientific calculator for the first time, might ask: 'What is the SIN key for?' One response to this would be to say that sines are used for calculations involving right-angled triangles, define what sine is and then explain how it is used. An alternative response would be to say: 'Enter some numbers and see what you happens when you use the SIN key.' This enables children to explore the significance of the numbers generated by their calculator and from this definitions and applications can be developed. The worksheet shown in Figure 7.4 was designed as a fairly structured starting point which reflects this latter style of response. It provides the sort of manageable approach which a mentor might suggest to a student whose previous experience of this topic has been traditional in style both in terms of mathematical content and presentation.

The links to right-angled triangles can be developed through asking questions about the kind of triangle shown in Figure 7.5a. Children can, for example, be challenged to use the information Figure 7.5 provides to solve a typical problem of the form: 'How far up a wall does an 8 metre ladder reach if it makes an angle of 70 degrees with the ground?' With such an approach, precise definitions and formalizing of the procedures, perhaps as indicated in Figure 7.6, comes rather late in a sequence of lessons, in contrast to the way in which many students will have learnt their own mathematics both at school and beyond.

It is important that student-teachers are introduced to alternative ideas relating to a wide range of curriculum topics. These should relate both to varying styles of teaching and learning and to varying ways of defining mathematical concepts and solving problems, whether they be routine like calculating sides in a right-angled triangle or more subtle like finding a function to generate an unfamiliar sequence of numbers. The teacher's ability to respond to the unexpected by asking an apt question or suggesting a new line of enquiry will only be developed if they are constantly seeking to widen their own

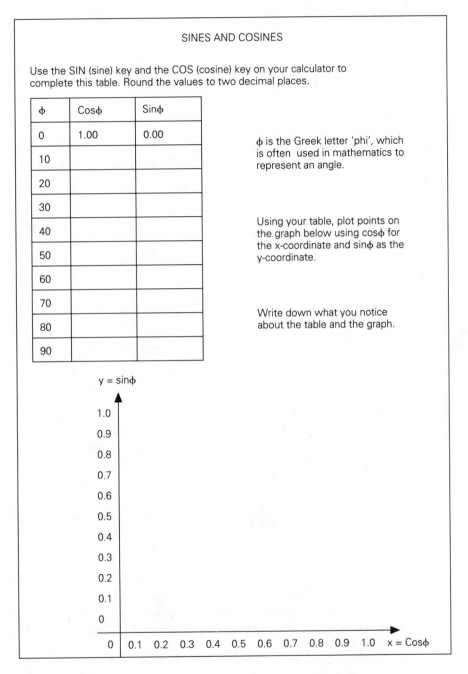

SINES AND COSINES

Use the SIN (sine) key and the COS (cosine) key on your calculator to complete this table. Round the values to two decimal places.

φ	Cosφ	Sinφ
0	1.00	0.00
10		
20		
30		
40		
50		
60		
70		
80		
90		

φ is the Greek letter 'phi', which is often used in mathematics to represent an angle.

Using your table, plot points on the graph below using cosφ for the x-coordinate and sinφ as the y-coordinate.

Write down what you notice about the table and the graph.

y = sinφ

1.0
0.9
0.8
0.7
0.6
0.5
0.4
0.3
0.2
0.1
0

0   0.1   0.2   0.3   0.4   0.5   0.6   0.7   0.8   0.9   1.0   x = Cosφ

Figure 7.4

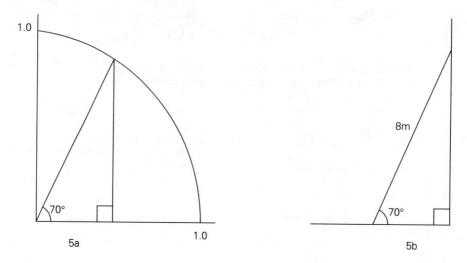

Figure 7.5

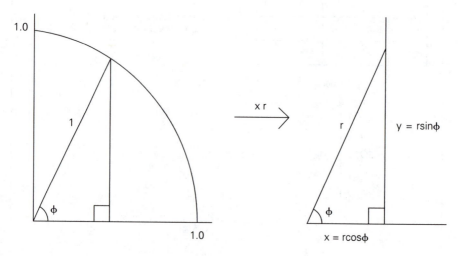

Figure 7.6

understanding of the mathematics they are helping children to learn and at the same time questioning the effectiveness of their teaching styles and trying to develop and improve them.

Again there are questions that the mentor can ask which will promote discussion and encourage the student to think and question their own pre-conceptions. The questions below are prompted by the example of sines and cosines, but the same questioning needs to be encouraged about a wide range of topics from the mathematics curriculum.

- What useful prior knowledge do you expect children to have?
- What are the key ideas that children need to understand about sines and cosines?
- What do you expect children to be able to do with that knowledge?
- What written work might children do, both to practise the skills of solving right-angled triangles and to extend their thinking in other ways?
- How does a topic like this help to fulfil aspects of Attainment Target 1 of the National Curriculum?
- How would you expect children to respond to the request to 'write down what you notice about the table and the graph' and how would you follow up their ideas?
- What extensions of this topic are possible?
- Are there advantages in introducing tangent before sine and cosine?
- Can you relate research on children's understanding of similarity and ratio to alternative ways of defining sine and cosine?*

These questions could be used as a basis for planning, observation or collaborative teaching as discussed in Chapter 6.

A Recurring Theme

	26		26
	x 25		x 25
(7a)	70	(7b)	130
			520
			650

Figure 7.7

Barrie, a student-teacher working alongside a teacher using the SMILE scheme, found a pupil, Jill, who had done the calculation shown in Diagram 7a.[†] Barrie established that Jill had said: '5 × 6 = 30; put down 0 and carry 3; 2 × 2 = 4; 4 + 3 = 7.' He then asked what 10 × 25 would be and was instantly told 250, from which it was clear to Jill that 70 could not be correct. Barrie's next step was to demonstrate a correct procedure set out as shown in Diagram 7b, and this enabled Jill to proceed with some similar examples.

This critical incident was recounted by Barrie to his mentor and provided a fruitful starting point for discussion. In Barrie's terms Jill did not know how

---

* See, for example, Open University (1988).
† SMILE stands for Secondary Mathematics Individualized Learning Experience. Details are available from the SMILE Centre, 108a Lancaster Road, London W11 1QS.

to carry out a standard procedure correctly and had not realized that an error had been made. He therefore first convinced her that there was an error by asking a pertinent question, and then gave a correct procedure. The mentor felt that Barrie could be encouraged to take a wider view of what might be achieved through such an encounter. Discussion therefore focused on how Jill could build on her, obviously secure, knowledge that $10 \times 25 = 250$ to arrive at an answer to 26×25. Barrie was asked to think of how he would do this himself in his head and having thought of one approach to think of another. Would Jill have learnt something of value by being asked to think in the same way?

I observed a lesson being taken by a student, Carl. He was giving a Year 7 class a set of ten mental questions at the start of the lesson. After the questions he gave out the answers and chose to make some comments about one of the questions: $16 + 19 + 13$. He said: 'The best way to do this is to do the 10s first. That makes 30, and then 6 and 9 is 15, and 3 makes 18. So it is 48 altogether.' While Carl was commenting on another question, I overheard a boy nearby in a heated whispered comment to his friend say: 'I didn't do it like that. I said 6 and 3 is 9, then two 9s are 18 and then add on the 30.' I recounted the boy's comment to Carl after the lesson. We discussed the value of giving pupils the opportunity to share their ideas with others and how they, and the teacher, have much to learn from what each has to say.

The Non-Statutory Guidance to the National Curriculum says:

> The ability to use mental arithmetic in everyday life and work is very important. This includes the vital skills of estimating results in advance, and of checking mentally for accuracy and reasonableness. (NCC, 1989)

Opportunities for using mental methods of calculation arise constantly in the classroom and are a theme which the mentor can help the student-teacher recognize and learn how to develop through incidental questions and discussion. Valuable material on this topic will be found in the Mathematical Association's book *Mental Methods in Mathematics: A First Resort*, which draws attention to the value of encouraging children and their teachers to talk about and share their methods of mental calculation as a way of extending their understanding and skills.

The mentor's questions can provoke the student-teachers to think about their own methods of calculation as well as how to encourage children to develop their own powers to the full. For example:

- How would you calculate 26×25 in your head?
- Can you think of several different ways of doing it?
- How do you follow up after giving children some mental calculations to do?
- How do you react to children's mistakes?

- What is the effect on children of presenting questions in the form of a test?

Learning Mathematics with a Microcomputer

The mentor and other mathematics teachers can help a student develop awareness of resources such as practical apparatus, calculators and computers by a wide use of these in lessons which the student observes. The use of computers, although emphasized by the National Curriculum, can still be a problem area for many teachers, and students need help in addressing the complexity of issues which computer use raises. They need experience of the computer laboratory, working with whole classes on LOGO, or using spreadsheets or databases as tools for exploring mathematics.*

Many mathematics classrooms have a single micro available, and students need to become aware of its possibilities. The following example highlights one such possibility. The focus of attention is a micro with a short program that acts as an input–output machine. The short dialogue could have arisen either as part of a class discussion or in a discussion with a small group of children.

Teacher:	Somebody suggest a small number.
Pupil:	Seven. ['7' is entered on the screen and '56' appears.]
Teacher:	Any comments?
Pupil:	It's seven eights.
Teacher:	Another number?
Pupil:	Four.
Teacher:	What do you think will happen?
Pupil:	Twenty, because it's four fives. ['4' is entered on the screen and '44' appears.] Oh, four elevens. It's not right.
Teacher:	Let's try another number. ['9' is entered on the screen and '54' appears.]

Several more numbers were tried and the results, with suggested factorizations, were summarized on the board as the discussion proceeded, making it possible for the pupils to make conjectures about which numbers could be tested with further examples. Eventually they were satisfied that one factor was the input number and the second factor was found by making the two factors together 'add up to 15'.

$$7 \longrightarrow 56 = 7 \times 8$$
$$4 \longrightarrow 44 = 4 \times 11$$
$$9 \longrightarrow 54 = 9 \times 6$$

* For a detailed discussion of some of these issues see Mathematical Association, 1992b.

Subsequent discussion led on to seeing that the function could be expressed as x(15 − x) in terms of the input number x, and at this point the teacher revealed the program on the screen as:

```
10 INPUT X
20 PRINT X*(15 − X)
30 RUN
```

Two further problems were then suggested for the class to work on using their calculators: to find what input gave the maximum output and what input(s) would give an output of 40.

In discussing such a lesson with a student teacher who was present the mentor's questions can help the student to reflect upon and learn from what has been observed and to develop the ability to ask their own questions.

- What were the intentions of the lesson?
- How did the micro contribute to the success of what was done?
- Would the same type of activity be possible without a micro?
- What was the teacher's role in this lesson?
- What knowledge of micros is required to do something like this?
- How could the ideas of this lesson be developed and extended?

There is extensive software now available which could be used to stimulate classroom activity. Students might be encouraged to use some of this with small groups of pupils, either within a class, or withdrawn from a class, over a series of lessons. In this way the student gains familiarity and confidence with computer potential and pupils are offered stimulating learning experiences to complement other work.

Conclusion

In the National Curriculum for Mathematics, Attainment Targets 2 to 5 relate to content, whereas Attainment Target 1, concerned with using and applying mathematics, relates to what are often referred to as *process skills*. While it may have been necessary, in order to draw attention to the importance of the process element, to present this as a separate target it has the unfortunate effect of encouraging a central aspect of mathematics to be seen as something separate, rather than an all-pervading element that should influence and draw upon all the content targets.

HMI in their report on the first year of the National Curriculum indicated that two of the main issues related to planning the curriculum are how to:

- use Programmes of Study to provide a broad and balanced mathematics curriculum for all pupils in an integrated rather than a fragmented way;

- ensure that problem solving, investigative activities, practical work and the use of calculators and microcomputers are central to the mathematics curriculum rather than 'bolt-on extras'.

This echoes the statement in the Non-Statutory Guidance that perhaps the 'single most significant challenge for the teaching of mathematics' is 'to develop a teaching and learning approach in which the uses and applications of mathematics permeate and influence all work in mathematics'.

Although there is a widespread acceptance of such aims, it is not an easy matter to put them into practice on a wide scale. As Peter Gates points out in Chapter 2, many student-teachers start their training with a very narrow content-based view of mathematics and of the ways in which it is learnt. The mentor is in a powerful position to influence their attitudes to the curriculum by increasing their awareness of a wide range of approaches and resources through providing opportunities for observing, discussing and trying out alternatives, and by encouraging them to reflect on their experiences in the classroom.

The examples in this chapter do not provide a grand overview of the mathematics curriculum, but they have indicated a variety of ways in which a mentor can use the opportunities that arise in any school to encourage reflection about children learning mathematics and the role of the mentor in promoting this.

References

HART, K. (Ed.) (1981) *Children's Understanding of Mathematics: 11–16*, London, John Murray.

HMI (1991) *Mathematics Key Stages 1 and 3: A Report by HM Inspectorate on the First Year, 1989–90*, London, HMSO.

MATHEMATICAL ASSOCIATION (1992a) *Mental Methods in Mathematics: A First Resort*, Leicester, Mathematical Association.

MATHEMATICAL ASSOCIATION (1992b) *Micros in the Mathematics Curriculum*, Leicester, Mathematical Association.

NATIONAL CURRICULUM COUNCIL (NNC) (1989) *Mathematices Non-Statutory Guidance*, York, NCC.

OPEN UNIVERSITY (1988) 'Preparing to teach ratio', *Project Mathematics Update*, Milton Keynes, Open University.

Chapter 8

The Wider Curriculum

Barrie Galpin and Simon Haines

Student-teachers need to consider issues of learning and teaching beyond those relating directly to teaching mathematics in their own classroom. Much of the wider school curriculum is beyond the scope of this book, but two areas of concern for the mathematics mentor are addressed here — those of equal opportunities and of cross-curricular links.

Introduction

Much of the book has addressed issues which are specific to mathematics classrooms without specifically addressing issues in the wider curriculum. It is the purpose of this chapter to consider wider issues in two areas, those of equal opportunities, and of cross-curricular work. In dealing with them we will endeavour to set them in the context of the mathematics classroom and focus on aspects which impinge on the role of the mathematics mentor. We will point out some ways in which the mentor may be able to raise wider curriculum issues with student-teachers during the school practice. Much has previously been written* about the way in which these issues have importance for mathematics teachers and for teachers in general and we shall not try here to duplicate this.

First we would like to stress that it is highly likely that each individual school will have an explicit policy on many of these wider issues. It could therefore be part of the mentor's responsibilities to ensure that these policies are brought to the attention of the student. This will need to be done close to the beginning of the practice in a formal manner, either by the mentor or perhaps by one of the senior staff in the school. The mentor will then be able to make mention of the school policies in the context of situations that arise naturally or are manufactured for that purpose as the practice develops.

---

* We have provided an extensive bibliography at the end of the chapter. These sources should be available through the HE Department library even if they are not part of the school's own staff resources.

In Chapter 3, Sue Sanders discussed how one's personal philosophy of mathematics teaching influences one's practice. We would also like to begin with some thoughts about why we teach and why we attach great importance to wider curriculum issues. The opening words of the Cockcroft Report (1982) are:

> There can be no doubt that there is general agreement that every child should study mathematics at school; indeed the study of mathematics, together with that of English, is regarded by most people as being essential.

As mathematics teachers we certainly agree, but is that the only reason why we teach? Certainly we believe that mathematics is a powerful means of communication and we want pupils to be empowered. Certainly we want pupils to develop the mathematical understanding and skills that they will need in adult life. Certainly we hope that we can help pupils to derive enjoyment from the subject, and to appreciate its beauty. However, we want much more besides. We also want our pupils to become caring, sensitive, critical, challenged and challenging individuals.

We recognize that this is a continuous process that will take a lifetime and we will use the metaphor of a *journey along a road* to describe it. We know that we ourselves are only travellers on this journey and are aware that sometimes it is all too easy to stop travelling, feeling that we've arrived in pleasant countryside, only to realize suddenly that there is further to go yet. However, as teachers we can help adolescents, at perhaps the most formative time of their lives, to join us on the journey. When we see this happening we can derive immense satisfaction from our teaching, helping us to persevere on our own journeys. As teachers of mathematics our particular means of achieving these aims lies in the mathematics classroom and we can use that medium to provide a context within which our contact with pupils can help them to develop as people.

In our role as mentors of student-teachers we have similar aims, both mathematical and more general, to those we have as teachers of mathematics. The mathematical issues may be different with less need to deal with new mathematical content *per se*. It is often the case that students who have studied mathematics in an academic way at a high level may not come to appreciate the beauties of the the subject until they begin to teach. It seems that a mathematics degree may often give less scope for creative activity in the subject than can be supplied within school classrooms. Many practising teachers who have graduated in mathematics testify to the fact that it was in their education year that they really fell in love with their subject. As mentors we may have the privilege of being matchmakers in a love affair between students and the subject they will teach.

However, just as we have wider aims for our pupils, so also for our students. We hope that they too will be on the way to becoming caring, sensitive, critical, challenged and challenging individuals. It is always important to remember the wide spectrum of experience in the students who arrive to work with us. No two will have the same history or be at the same point on the journey. Some will be well along the way and may themselves be able to guide and support us. Others will need more guidance from us or even need encouragement to undertake the journey.

Progress on this journey is not necessarily a function of age of course. For example, one pair of students with whom one of us worked consisted of a 22-year-old straight from school and university, paired for the teaching practice with a mature student who was intending to move into teaching having given up a successful career in industry. Clearly the one had far more life experience than the other, yet it seemed that the younger one had made far more progress along the journey that we have been describing. It was he who cared about the children he taught, treated their individuality with respect and was able to question and work on his own attitudes and behaviour. The older student found it far harder to appreciate the need to develop in this area and to question his own attitudes and, as others saw it, bias.

How, as mentors, can we influence students to progress? It is tempting to think that our example alone will be sufficient to set them in the right direction but it is often the case that we will have to raise issues explicitly with students. Later in the chapter we will recount some experience of this and offer suggestions of ways in which this can be done in an assertive but non-threatening way. There is clearly little place for preaching in this sphere of our work and we must strike a balance between passivity and overactivity. Of course we hope that by encouraging students on their journeys they will in turn adopt similar aims with their pupils. By raising issues specifically we hope that they will come to realize the importance of the wider curriculum alongside the mathematical one.

Equal Opportunities

It is of major concern among mathematics teachers and some of the wider public that girls tend to underachieve in mathematics. This is also true of some other groups, identified by class or race, who may also underachieve across a wider academic spectrum. Consideration of how a teacher might contribute to, or help counteract, these trends should be an important part of the development of a student-teacher's practice.

Students who arrive in secondary classrooms often find themselves in an unfamiliar social setting. Quite apart from the age difference between themselves and their pupils there are often other social factors which may put up potential barriers. Student-teachers will often have values and prejudices which have been influenced by their own backgrounds and educational success and they will need to be aware of these. For example, the student will almost certainly assume the value of and the need for education, something which is not necessarily shared by all pupils and parents. Whatever their background, as student-teachers they will all have achieved a measure of academic success and this will often be in stark contrast to many of the young people they will teach.

There are also likely to be differences of race or ethnic background. In the UK so far, student-teachers are most likely to be white, whereas in our multicultural society there may be substantial numbers of pupils of other races or ethnic backgrounds. Conversely, the slowly increasing number of student-teachers from ethnic minority groups may find themselves teaching in schools where the majority of children are white. Another difference between students and pupils which occurs less frequently but which may be particularly acute is where there are physical disabilities. Finally there will be differences between students and pupils in terms of their gender and sexuality. There will be students who will feel more at ease with pupils of one gender than another and, similarly, pupils who will relate more easily to either male or female students and teachers.

Of course the differences which are apparent for the students are also applicable for their mentors. In recent years, schools have been increasingly aware that they must address equal opportunities issues and many teachers will have attended courses aimed at increasing their awareness in these areas. Therefore many mentors will feel that they are some way towards awareness of issues of equal opportunities even though they will probably feel, like us, that there are still great distances to go.

It would be good (but probably unrealistic) to assume that most students will be well on the way to perceptive self-evaluation. The way to encourage this is certainly not by means of a didactic, heavy-handed approach but by means of more subtle methods. A particularly appropriate time to raise these issues is when students are observing mentors' lessons or when they are team teaching together. However, it is easy to be too subtle; it may not be enough for students just to observe 'good practice'. It may well be necessary to make the practice and issues explicit, drawing attention to the school policy statement in the course of prior or subsequent discussion.

One student was planning a series of lessons around the well-known 'Frogs' investigation and outlined to her mentor how she intended to organize this. At one point she planned to form two teams. When the mentor asked why there was a boys' team and a girls' team the student replied that she had not really thought about it, but that it seemed to be an easy way of dividing the class into two. The mentor asked whether the student would ever divide the class according to their colour if that were convenient and the student was horrified at the idea. The mentor was then able to explain that she tried never to divide the class in such a way and was able to explain that such a decision could lend credence to perceptions of gender differences in the learning of mathematics. The student was happy to accept another way of dividing the class into two and then became aware that she had been unconsciously treating boys and girls differently throughout her teaching, for example by releasing girls first at the end of the lesson, directing questions specifically at and accepting contributions from one group or the other.

This incident shows that it is often possible for mentors to draw attention to such behaviour in a way that can encourage the student's own self-awareness.

In fact, research shows that there appear to be gender differences in terms of confidence in mathematics, expectations of achievement and preferred ways of working. One example of this is reported by a 12-year-old girl in the book, *Girls into Mathematics*:

> It was the start of the new school year in a secondary school. The boys and girls were lined up outside their first mathematics class. As the teacher supervised them filing in he said: 'Girls, sit at the back because mathematics is not such an important subject for you as it is for the boys.' (Open University, 1986)

There are still misconceptions existing which portray mathematics as a boys' subject. In the classroom it is important for all teachers of mathematics to be aware of this stereotyping both in ourselves and, unfortunately, in many of our pupils. We need to be continually asking ourselves whether we have different expectations of pupils of different gender, expectations which are based upon our own misconceived preconceptions about boys' and girls' abilities in mathematics. We also need to be aware that many of our pupils, by the time they reach us in secondary schools, may also have adopted these misconceptions about the mathematical ability of the sexes. Pupils' behaviour, responses to the teacher, willingness to ask questions, need for support and the commonly found obsession with neatness rather than content of work can often be explained as manifestations of gender bias and are often reinforced by insensitive classroom practice.

These gender issues which exist in the mathematics classroom are well documented, but there are also a number of racial, cultural and class issues which are specific to mathematics. For example, the mathematics we teach is embedded in the traditions of western culture with the historical contributions of mathematicians from other cultures often going unrecognized. One example, pointed out by George Joseph, in his book *The Crest of the Peacock*, concerns the triangular pattern of numbers ascribed to Blaise Pascal, which was actually being used by the Chinese many years before its appearance in Europe. We note, ironically, that we have named the European mathematician, but not the Chinese one! As the example shows, Western European names tend to dominate mathematics, implying that it 'belongs to' Europe, while other important mathematicians are forgotten. George Joseph's book is one of a growing number of works which attempt to start to redress this balance.

Parental expectations in mathematics can be a very strong influence and teachers have reported that this can often be particularly acute in some Asian families where additional pressure may be put on pupils, particularly the boys, to succeed in what is seen as a particularly important subject. However, although there may be evidence of this occurring in some Asian families, we do need to be particularly careful with such generalizations which can quickly lead to unjustified stereotyping.

Within the statistics part of the mathematics curriculum there are often opportunities to raise equal opportunities issues explicitly. Such situations do need to be handled with care, but can provide possibilities for issues to be raised and commented upon. Examples might include an investigation of people's food preferences comparing the views of different ethnic groups, or an investigation of people's television viewing habits comparing the views of boys and girls. Experienced teachers will appreciate the need for care with topics such as the occupations of pupils' parents and family size, but student-teachers may overlook the potential difficulties, for example, for pupils from one-parent families. They may also be unaware of pupils' sensitivities — about height and weight for example. The mentor may need to monitor the sort of investigations that students undertake with their pupils, encouraging them to anticipate possible difficulties so as to either prepare sensitively for them or avoid the topic.

It will almost certainly be the case that the HE Department will be seeking to raise awareness during the course. How this is done is itself an interesting question. Do equal opportunities permeate the course as a whole or does it have a separate slot where the issues are raised? Probably the answer is that both are necessary. The provision of equal opportunity in the classroom is not solely a matter of eliminating bias and prejudice, however. It is also about creating appropriate learning experiences for all children, whatever their mathematical achievement so far, so that they may all have access to a wide range of mathematics and chances to learn more. This requires attention to be paid to individual states of knowledge and responses to different ways of teaching. (Much of this book illustrates an equal opportunities approach in this sense, both for teachers and for mentors.) We hope that equal opportunity awareness permeates our practice but is also raised explicitly.

Our task as mentors is to find ways of raising our own awareness and that of our students to these issues. In order to do this we can study our own existing classroom practice and the experience and attitudes of the students and of ourselves. For example:

An experienced teacher became aware that Stephen, a boy in a Year 10 mixed-ability class who could neither read nor write, was far ahead of everyone else in the group in calculating the number of paths from the origin to any point on a coordinate grid. He also had an efficient general explanation of his solutions. The teacher had introduced the problem in a practical way and the boy's success made her aware of the need to provide more obstacle-free mathematical situations for him and others in future.

The need for critical self-awareness is paramount and for this to be effective there must be a professional relationship and mutual trust established between mentors and students, a realization by both parties that both are endeavouring to progress towards greater awareness.

How do we detect, for instance, gender bias in our classrooms? Certainly the presence of another teacher acting as a non-teaching observer may help. One of us has had the opportunity to observe other teachers' lessons and then to ask them about their perceptions of the relative amounts of time that they have spent with girls and with boys. Very often their perception is of parity, whereas to the observer it appeared that one group was getting a disproportionate amount of time at the expense of the others. Similarly there may be questions about the nature of the interaction:

- Who initiates it?
- How is time spent with an individual?
- What expectations are placed upon the individual during that conversation?
- Are the answers to these questions affected by the gender of the pupils, their ethnic origin, or their perceived ability?

It may be that we will want to spend more or less time or energy with particular individuals or groups and there may be very good reasons for doing so. It may also prove important to observe behaviour away from the teacher. Is anyone being ridiculed, treated as a fetcher and carrier, ignored, name-called, expected to provide answers for others or otherwise being prevented from taking a full part in the lesson?

If student and mentor are observing each other's lessons for such purposes there may well be very positive benefits in explaining this explicitly to the pupils. We may also wish to take the opportunity to point out to our pupils that the principle of equal opportunities for all determines much of what is done in the classroom. This is why pupils are not allowed to shout out, why we organize groups in a particular way or why we use particular curriculum materials. Our aim is to allow as many pupils as possible to get involved, have ideas, make mistakes, and feel successful with mathematics without fear of ridicule or stereotyping. We also hope that, through this, they also learn to value each other.

Specific observation by someone other than the teacher may highlight inequalities and lead to their exploration, but it is important that observer and teacher agree on the focus of the observation beforehand. There may be positive benefits for such observation to be carried out by the student in the mentor's classroom early in the practice, rather than observation of the student by the mentor. In that way we can signal that we as mentors are also wishing to raise our own awarenesses and it is a way of raising with students an issue such as gender bias in a way that is non-threatening to them. For example, while students are observing the mentor's lesson they could be asked to help the mentor's own gender awareness by counting the number of times boys and girls respond to questions in class discussion, or how many times the mentor picks boys and girls to answer particular questions.

Of course by doing this we will be putting ourselves in a position that may appear threatening to us. Will we be able to cope with a suggestion that we may be exhibiting bias? Do we really want to know? How will it feel to be discussing this with someone who has a fraction of our teaching experience? Such questions may throw a new light upon our understanding of the mentoring role. It is possible that conflict of view may arise from this shared reflection, and our relationship with the student must be able to sustain mutual tolerance and respect for each other's beliefs.

It is not only a matter of trying to ensure equality of opportunity for those whom we teach, there is also the question of ensuring that our attitudes and the resources that we use are free of prejudice. It is perfectly possible to practise gender discrimination in single-sex schools, just as one may exhibit racial prejudice in classrooms where only a single racial group is represented. The attitudes and practices of teachers, students and pupils in such circumstances will need to be monitored, and again, when another adult is present in the classroom, there are opportunities, given the right sort of professional relationship, for such issues to be raised. By inviting students to look out for instances of prejudice as they observe mentor's lessons and in the resources that we use, we can raise these issues in the student's consciousness.

As well as taking advantage of the opportunity for shared reflection provided by having another teacher in the classroom, it is also vital to develop techniques by which we and the students can increase self-awareness so that, when there is not the luxury of a colleague observing, we can still find opportunities to reflect upon our teaching. For example, it is very easy to take advantage of having additional assistance by asking the student who is observing a lesson to spend extra time with a child at the extremes of the ability range and who apparently needs individual help. However, a more far reaching and long-term strategy could be to suggest that the student assists the mentor to establish a method of providing assistance for the particular child, a method which both student and mentor can then adopt when in the future they find themselves unsupported in the classroom. For example:

> During his course, one student was able to spend several periods of up to an hour with pupils who had difficulty in expressing their 'workings out' on paper. The insights that he gained from one-to-one contact helped him understand more about their inherent difficulties and helped the mathematics department to learn more about the special needs of individuals and how to meet them.

As mentors it is our responsibility to ensure that all the issues already mentioned in this section are faced by students. Direct experience from real classroom incidents that arise during the teaching practice may be the most fruitful method for exploring this. However, this may not always be possible and other means may need to be employed.

There is a wealth of human resources within schools which can be valuably exploited. This may involve students spending time in class with teachers from other subject areas, attending equal opportunities courses or INSET, or spending time with school support agencies. It may well be possible for the student to discuss the school's equal opportunities policy with a member of the senior management team.

Equal opportunities cannot be separated from classroom practice as a whole; they are not different issues. We would argue strongly that teachers who are actively examining their practice from an equal opportunities aspect will benefit not only in this area, but also in their classroom teaching as a whole.

In this section we have talked about how mathematics teachers can play a part, through mathematics, in the equal opportunities curriculum of the school. Now we are going to look at the wider academic curriculum and the place of mathematics in it.

Mathematics across the Curriculum

We have already made it clear that teaching is about helping pupils develop in a wider sense than just as mathematicians. This cannot be achieved if the subject, and its teachers, exist in isolation. Teachers can learn from colleagues in other subject areas just as mathematics can be found in many different contexts. We would identify two particular ways in which mathematics across the curriculum may be addressed during the teaching practice experience. The first is by means of students taking the opportunity to visit lessons of subjects other than mathematics and the second by means of their becoming engaged in collaborative work with colleagues from other disciplines.

It is unfortunately the case that for many practising teachers there is little opportunity to visit the classrooms of colleagues from other disciplines, but during the teaching practice there may be a time when this can be achieved. If it is to be of particular use the programme of visits needs to be planned carefully, with particular objectives which are made clear both to students and to the teachers whose classrooms they visit. Students may be particularly interested in science, IT or special needs teaching, but we also suggest that experience of drama, art or language classrooms could provide rich food for thought about how to involve and motivate children.

Frequently students in their initial few days in the school are able to shadow particular children or groups in order to get a 'child's eye view' of the school. This may be too early in the practice to expect students to be able to focus on mathematics across the curriculum although they may notice particular incidents or attitudes which can be discussed with the tutor. The following anecdote is a case in point:

> A student-teacher was shadowing a group of Year 10 pupils for a day and the first two lessons were mathematics and chemistry. In the mathematics lesson the teacher was explaining how to use and solve simultaneous equations. By the end of the session, it seemed to the student that most pupils had experienced a significant degree of success. In the following chemistry lesson the group carried out an experiment and were then brought together by the teacher to analyse the results. The student was again impressed by the science teacher's exposition, which led eventually to two equations with two unknowns written on the board. 'How do we solve this then?' asked the teacher. A silence fell to be followed by general agreement from the class that they had never done anything like that before. The student smiled to herself and remembered what they had been doing an hour beforehand, but she seemed to be the only one who did.

Anecdotes such as this highlight how mathematical content is to be found in many other curriculum areas, but how difficult the required transference of knowledge and skills can be. On top of this, many of the processes that we expect our pupils to develop are likely to be also required in other subject areas.

So what particular opportunities and challenges does this offer to mathematics mentors? We have already (we hope!) helped our students to become aware of a coherent and cohesive model for the mathematics curriculum. We may well have encouraged them to adopt a critical stance in relation to it but, assuming that this is the first tangible school experience for the students, such a state of mind will have been difficult to achieve. However, by providing opportunities for students to observe work in a different curriculum area we may be able to draw their attention to contrasting styles of teaching and learning. How, for example, is the problem of differentiated abilities tackled by the English department? What role does discussion play in promoting learning in art or technology? Are there opportunities for practical activities in humanities and modern languages and are these considered to be an integral part of the learning process? Such questions about the nature of teaching and learning are in addition to the more obvious ones such as how number skills are drawn upon and developed in science lessons and what knowledge and understanding of statistics is required in humanities. In this way it may be possible to encourage students to reflect not only on the uses of mathematics in different contexts, but also to become more critical of the mathematics curriculum itself, having gained a wider perspective of different styles of teaching and learning.

In addition to opening up possibilities to observe work in other subject disciplines, the extra teaching resource provided by the presence of student-teachers in the school can often allow sufficient flexibility for students and teachers from different subject areas to work collaboratively. The planning implications can be great, especially where communication between departments is not easy. In practice it may be that the mathematics mentor will be more likely to seek collaborative work with departments where there are already established links of this sort. On the other hand the presence of a student may act as the catalyst for interdepartmental cross-curricular work where none existed beforehand.

Working with mathematics in another curriculum area with non-mathematics specialists can provide rich learning opportunities for all those involved: pupils, students and teachers. If student-teachers are to undertake work of this type then clearly their own interests and enthusiasms may well affect the type of project chosen, as will the availability and willingness of other staff to be involved. Mentors may well be involved in the joint project but if this is not the case they will often need to assist the student in the initial contacts to be made with other staff and departments.

In some joint projects it would be easy to view the mathematics as providing a tool to be used within the other discipline. Examples might be projects linked to humanities where statistics are useful (such as smoking or advertising) or to technology or science where aspects of mathematics are necessary to solve problems (such as trigonometry for building bridges, graphs in representing relationships). Another project of this type might be one where a mathematics and geography teacher together planned a project on mapping and survey work. The danger with such projects is that they can reinforce the view (in students as well as pupils) that mathematics is *only* a tool, a service subject for other disciplines.

If, however, mathematics teachers take opportunities frequently to refer to other subjects when suggesting applications of mathematical ideas, this can be important in influencing pupils' perceptions of mathematics and its place in the curriculum. It may also be possible to invite other departments to collaborate in a project which arises from studying mathematics. For example, one of us has been involved in a collaborative project about the language of instruction with an English teacher where the project arose from work in mathematics on LOGO. Historians may be interested in working on a project on the history of calculating devices. Other departments might be involved in the establishment of a maths trail or in a real problem-solving project. Particularly useful collaboration may be possible between the mathematics and art departments, dealing for example with symmetry. Here there are opportunities for the two disciplines to stand in symbiotic association, providing each other with mutual support.

If we are to be able to assist in arranging such a project we will need to be clear beforehand what exactly the aims of such collaborative work may be. Students will need to decide what mathematical content is likely to be needed in the project and whether and at what stage this will have to be dealt with explicitly. Perhaps, more importantly, all those involved need to be clear about common processes that are being used. Is there a consistent philosophy being offered? Are the skills required very different?

In whatever way it is set up, cross-curricular work can provide enormous benefits for student-teachers, helping them to understand the way in which another department works and the way in which mathematics is viewed by specialists from other disciplines. It also offers the students the chance to gain wider and deeper insights about the nature of teaching and learning.

Conclusion

The period of teaching practice is a short time when there is an enormous range of new experiences for student-teachers to come to terms with. Clearly there will not be time to engage in detail in all the possible issues that this book and this chapter have identified. Mentors and students must necessarily choose to concentrate on particular issues according to their own circumstances and personal preferences. As we pointed out in the introduction we may be able to assist students to take a few small steps along a journey towards becoming caring, sensitive, critical, challenged and challenging individuals. We would do well to remember that we as mentors are only involved with the student's initial training. Although we can provide only a short experience of, for example, cross-curricular work, this may well provide the stimulus for future work of this nature by the newly qualified teacher. As mentors we are only agents in the students' initial stages of professional development.

It would be easy to view many of the issues which we have addressed in this chapter as being peripheral to the main responsibilities of the mathematics mentor. However, we would point again to the ideas which we expressed in the introduction. Do we really see our reasons for teaching extending beyond the mathematics to helping pupils to become more fulfilled individuals and valued members of society? Do we have similar aspirations for the students with whom we will be working? If so then the issues which we have dealt with here, far from being peripheral, will be of central importance, even if they often lie below the surface as the foundations of our day-to-day work as mathematics mentors.

References

ASCHER, M. (1991) *Ethnomathematics: A Multicultural View of Mathematical Ideas*, Pacific Grove, CA, Brooks/Cole Publishing Company.

ASHWORTH, F. *et al.* (1991) 'Maths trailing in Dorset', *Mathematics in School*, **20**, 1.

ASSOCIATION OF TEACHERS OF MATHEMATICS (1993) *Talking Maths, Talking Language*, Derby, ATM.

BARHAM, J. and BISHOP, A.J. (1991) 'Mathematics and the deaf child' in DURKIN, K. and

SHIRE, B. (Eds) *Language in Mathematical Education: Research and Practice*, Milton Keynes, Open University Press.

BISHOP, A.J. (1991) 'Teaching mathematics to ethnic minority pupils in secondary schools' in PIMM, D. and LOVE, E. (Eds) *Teaching and Learning School Mathematics*, London, Hodder and Stoughton.

COCKCROFT, W.H. (1982) *Mathematics Counts*, London, HMSO.

COLLINS, J. (1990) 'Road safety education in the National Curriculum? Let's start with mathematics', *Mathematics Teaching*, No. 133.

DALLOW, R. *et al.* (1991) 'Mathematics, science and technology: Springy Things Inc.', *Mathematics Teaching*, No. 135.

DILKE, O.A.W. (1987) *Reading the Past: Mathematics and Measurement*, London, British Museum.

EMBLEN, V. (1988) 'Asian children in schools' in PIMM, D. (Ed.) *Mathematics, Teachers and Children*, London, Hodder and Stoughton.

FAUVEL, J. (Ed.) (1990) 'History in the mathematics classroom', *The IREM Papers*, Vol. 1, Leicester, Mathematical Association.

FRANKENSTEIN, M. (1989) *Reiearning Mathematics: A Different Third R — Radical Math(s)*, London, Free Association Books.

GARDNER, H.J. (1991) 'How fast does the wind travel?: History in the primary mathematics classroom' in PIMM, D. and LOVE, E. (Eds) *Teaching and Learning School Mathematics*, London, Hodder and Stoughton.

GRAHAM, A. (1990) *Investigating Statistics: A Beginner's Guide*, London, Hodder and Stoughton.

HOYLES, C. and SUTHERLAND, R. (1989) *Logo Mathematics in the Classroom*, London, Routledge.

ISAACSON, Z. (1988) 'The marginalisation of girls in mathematics: Some causes and some remedies' in PIMM, D. (Ed.) *Mathematics, Teachers and Children*, London, Hodder and Stoughton.

JENNER, H. (1988) 'Mathematics for a multicultural society' in PIMM, D. (Ed.) *Mathematics, Teachers and Children*, London, Hodder and Stoughton.

JOSEPH, G.G. (1991) *The Crest of the Peacock*, London, Penguin.

LERMAN, S. (1992) 'Critical/humanistic mathematics education: A role for history?', *Multicultural Teaching*, **11**, 1, Autumn.

MACFARLANE, K. (1992) 'Girls into mathematics: An LEA based INSET initiative', *Mathematics in School*, **21**, 3.

MATHEMATICAL ASSOCIATION (1988) *Mathematics in a Multicultural Society*, Leicester, Mathematical Association.

MAXWELL, J. (1988) 'Hidden messages' in PIMM, D. (Ed.) *Mathematics, Teachers and Children*, London, Hodder and Stoughton.

NATIONAL COUNCIL OF TEACHERS OF MATHEMATICS (1989) *Historical Topics for the Mathematics Classroom*, Reston, VA, National Council of Teachers of Mathematics.

NICKSON, M. (1992) 'Towards a multicultural mathematics curriculum' in NICKSON, M. and LERMAN, S. (Eds) *The Social Context of Mathematics Education: Theory and Practice*, London, South Bank Press.

OPEN UNIVERSITY (1986) *Girls into Mathematics* (PM645) Milton Keynes, Open University.

OPEN UNIVERSITY (1990) *Working Mathematically within a Whole School Curriculum*, PM647F (video pack) Milton Keynes, Open University.

OPEN UNIVERSITY (1991) *Working Mathematically through Real Problem Solving*, PM647G (video pack), Milton Keynes, Open University.

PAECHTER, C. (1991) 'Holistic tasks in mathematics: Working with design and technology', *Mathematics Teaching*, No. 134.

PAJAK, J. (1990) 'The Stamford mathematics trail', *Mathematics in School*, **19**, 1.

POTTER, S. and HUGHES, P. (1990) *Vital Travel Statistics*, London, Transport 2000; (contains results from the 1985–6 National Travel Survey).

THE PROBLEM SOLVING SCHOOL GROUP (1988) *Towards the Problem Solving School*, Derby, Association of Teachers of Mathematics.

SHAN, S. and BAILEY, P. (1991) *Multiple Factors: Classroom Mathematics for Equality and Justice*, Stoke on Trent, Trentham.

THOMSON, M. (1991) 'Mathematics and dyslexia' in DURKIN, K. and SHIRE, B. (Eds) *Language in Mathematical Education: Research and Practice*, Milton Keynes, Open University Press.

URQUHART, D. and BALFOUR, G. (1992) 'Maths AIDS: Pastoral topics through maths — a case study', *Mathematics Teaching*, No. 138.

WALKERDINE, V. and the GIRLS IN MATHEMATICS UNIT (1989) *Counting Girls Out*, London, Virago Press.

ZAZLAVSKY, C. (1979) *Africa Counts*, New York, Lawrence Hill Books.

Chapter 9

Evaluation and Judgment

Maggie Crosson and Christine Shiu

One role of the mathematics mentor involves assessment and evaluation of student-teachers. This chapter looks at some of the practicalities and issues involved and presents case studies to illustrate them.

Introduction

Chapter 4 identified a number of roles which the mentor undertakes during the student's placement. In this chapter the focus is on another of these — mentor as *assessor* and *evaluator*. Evaluation is both ongoing and implicit in all mentoring acts. Assessment happens periodically when one pauses to take stock of the evaluative process, makes it more explicit, identifies and justifies judgments which are made, and reports conclusions. There can be some tension between moving between the obviously supportive aspects of being a mentor — even though this includes ongoing evaluation — and the judgmental aspects of writing reports and recommendations required for final assessment. However if the evaluative aspects of mentoring are recognized and worked on from the start such tensions can be fruitful and positive rather than threatening and negative.

Furthermore, in the evaluation and assessment of students, mentors are necessarily demonstrating something about these processes. Reflecting on their own experience of being assessed could give students valuable insight into the effect of being assessed. As a mentor you may wish to consider whether your assessment of the student-teacher is done according to the same principles which you apply to assessing the mathematics of your pupils. You may also like to share this issue at some stage with the student.

The Process of Evaluation

What Are The Purposes of Evaluation?

The purposes of evaluating students in their role as teachers include:

- to recognize developing awareness and highlight needs;
- to highlight and analyze successes;
- to identify problem areas and help formulate future targets;
- to inform judgments — assessments — about current or future suitability for mathematics teaching.

You may recognize these processes as similar to some forms of teacher appraisal.

In addition mentors need to work with students encouraging self-evaluation, negotiation about and involvement in their own progress. Because of their greater experience, mentors will be more aware of the range of possible issues students will need to address. Here the mentor plays an important role in helping the student clarify realistic achievable targets and identify helpful strategies to reach them.

In order for the practice to be as productive as possible the first three purposes need to be addressed explicitly throughout. Chapter 6 deals with evaluation of individual lessons. There is also an ongoing need for more generalized evaluation. In this chapter, we aim to draw together the issues to do with evaluation and show how they relate to the mentor's responsibilities in assessing a student's suitability for teaching.

Although final judgments are only made at the end of the practice they can be prepared for and worked towards by both mentor and student. The starting point is likely to be a list of criteria and principles for evaluation negotiated with the HE Department. However, it is unrealistic to expect a mentor to be completely objective in interpreting any criteria and more helpful to acknowledge that interpretation of them will depend on personal values and beliefs.

Apart from assessing the student-teacher, another aspect of evaluation in which the mentor will be directly involved is that of reflecting on the programme offered, and considering ways of improving it. This is unlikely to mean undertaking dramatic changes during the course of one student's practice. Rather it is about adapting plans and targets according to individual needs, and using insights gained from mentoring one student to inform the programme planned for future students.*

Guidelines for Evaluation

Since evaluation is a part of the practice as a whole, the student, mentor and tutor should all have access to all necessary information including aims, objectives and procedures for the course. Ideally all will have a role in shaping and developing these.

When you are preparing to act as mentor for a student it may be helpful

---

* See Chapter 4 for a discussion of evaluating students' needs and Chapter 2 for drawing on a tutor's wider experience of schools.

to start by reading the guidelines. (Don't hesitate to contact the HE Department if these do not arrive in good time!) These may be set out as a series of competencies, under headings such as:

- Preparation,
- Class management and organization,
- Teaching skills,
- Relationships with pupils,
- Relationships with staff,
- Personal and professional qualities,
- General suitability for teaching.

Such lists, of course, can never tell the whole story of what makes a competent teacher — still less what makes an outstanding one, but can be a good starting point for discussion. Eventually you may wish to introduce the student to the criteria. Since the totality of these might be overwhelming, this might valuably be done in a step by step way rather than all at once. Assessments will involve summative judgments and both parties are entitled to have explicit knowledge of the criteria to be applied.

Profiles

Students are likely to be involved in keeping a file or profile which is their personal record of the ongoing planning, reflective and evaluative processes discussed in Chapters 5 and 6, in particular the keeping of a log. These resources too are likely to have guidelines for their use and may be a way of introducing students to the evaluative criteria. The actual format of the profiles may vary between institutions but again, if their development has been shared, they will be valuable throughout the practice and can be referred to as judgments are made. An early discussion as to how the profile is to be used can help to clarify its value. It is also important, at this stage, to make a clear distinction between what is private writing and what is for overt sharing.

Planning for Evaluation

As a mentor you are likely to be a busy teacher with many responsibilities, so if evaluation is going to be as productive as possible, some preplanning and timetabling is called for. Below, one mentor gives her account of the preplanning she sees as necessary.

> I timetable a session with the student every week, for reflecting and evaluating. I also make sure we have somewhere where we can be undisturbed. I try to make sure there are no interruptions — sick

children, stock deliveries, cover for absent colleagues. So I will see the person who arranges cover to establish that I am not available at this particular time. In general I don't sacrifice long term important aims for short-term pressures which someone else can deal with.

I also like to sketch out a plan for evaluation activities and choose a sensible starting point. Part of the process in each session is to decide on the focus for the next session. It is important to have some plan so time is used well, but it is also important not to overplan in order to have time to deal with emerging issues and to respond to the particular needs of the student. Be prepared to abandon the whole plan in exceptional circumstances!

This teacher's own checklist for planning is included as Table 9.1 while Table 9.2 gives some suggestions for focuses for evaluation. Neither of these is prescriptive or exhaustive, but they are offered as possible starting points for discussion. For instance, in Table 9.1 it is assumed that the school has a professional tutor, someone who has an overview of general staff development.

Beliefs, Values and Attitudes

Teachers — and mentors — demonstrate their values implicitly in the way that they work and by the qualities they stress and reward.* It is not always easy, however, to articulate these, though it can be useful and illuminating to try to do so. One mentor when challenged to describe her notion of a good teacher gave the following response.

A good teacher is a collector and explorer. You collect ideas that you observe from other people, read about, hear about in meetings and staffroom discussions, and you explore strategies and ideas by trying them out and seeing what happens.

Often we take beliefs and values so much for granted that we only become aware of them when they are violated or challenged. The evaluation tasks become much more difficult when student and mentor have very different experiences and beliefs. However differences can be fruitful if there is enough trust to support a free and frank exchange of views and both sides are prepared to learn. If, however, people are inflexible and unwilling or unable to explain their philosophy, then their ability to evaluate will be limited

A young idealistic teacher believing passionately in 'mathematics for all' and 'cooperative learning' came in for criticism at the beginning of his career. He reported:

---

* Teachers' beliefs about mathematics, and the effects of these on mathematics teaching, are explored more fully in Chapter 3.

Table 9.1

PLANNING FOR EVALUATION

Before the start of the practice:

- make sure you have any guidelines for evaluation and profiling from the HE Department;
- read the guidelines, noting down any points that need clarifying;
- timetable evaluation sessions in a suitable room;
- see person who arranges cover for absent colleagues;
- delegate responsibility for dealing with other pressures during evaluation sessions;
- note down a rough plan for evaluation sessions using the guidelines if you find these useful;
- choose the focus for the first evaluation session;
- plan the first evaluation session leaving enough time to discuss emerging issues and to negotiate the focus for the second session with the student-teacher;
- check arrangements with the professional tutor.

During the practice:

- look through your rough plan and amend it if necessary depending on the strengths and weaknesses of the student;
- record each evaluation session and plan the focus of the next one with the student (copies to student and tutor?);
- discuss the student's progress and observations made with other members of staff in the department (and other departments if appropriate);
- discuss with tutor from awarding body, especially any doubts or anxieties;
- consult with professional tutor or other helpful member of staff if appropriate;
- half-way through the practice reread the guidelines for evaluation and your notes. Are there successes that you have not acknowledged yet? Are there areas of concern that you have not raised? Note these down and plan your response.

Towards the end of the practice:

- collect together observations made by other members of staff;
- look through your own notes and records;
- draft your final report;
- discuss your draft with the student and amend if necessary;
- send a copy of the final report to the awarding body, give one to the student and file one copy in school;
- you may find a copy of the report and some of your records or notes useful if you are asked to write references in the future.

After the practice:

- give yourself time to reflect on what happened during the practice and make notes which will help you plan for mentoring your next student-teacher.

Table 9.2

Professional qualities
Working as a member of a team/department.
Contributing ideas, cooperation, accepting advice. Awareness of and cooperation with school policy and ethos.
Relationships with other teaching and non-teaching staff. Politeness and reliability.

Preparation
Content of lessons, variety, stimulus, use of equipment, aims.

Evaluation of lessons
Recognizing successes, setting targets, checking assumptions, exploring alternatives, recording own progress.

Organization and management
Smooth and efficient running of the classroom, managing resources, sharing time between pupils effectively and fairly, helping pupils to manage their time efficiently.

Relationships with pupils
Gaining respect and trust. Making pupils aware that their progress is recognized and valued. Dealing with problems in a constructive way, encouraging pupils to share their anxieties, being perceived as fair and appropriately assertive. Personal style and pupil perceptions.

Group work
Encouraging group work. Decision-making and planning. Sharing and communication of ideas. Division of tasks.Working efficiently and cooperatively.

Possible topics for evaluation.

Assessment of pupils
Recognizing and recording achievement, setting targets, self-assessment, marking and record keeping.

General teaching skills
Communicating effectively, encouraging discussion, arousing enthusiasm and maintaining pupil involvement, providing positive feedback.

Comparison of teaching approaches
Ability to observe differences in styles, theory and organization between teachers in the school. Reflecting back to personal experience as a pupil. Checking assumptions made. Distinguishing/ discriminating between ideas/strategies observed.

Mathematics
Range, scope and suitability of mathematics used.

Equal opportunities
Consideration of the needs of all abilities, genders, races, etc.

Encouraging investigational approaches
Creating an environment where pupils feel able to take risks. Helping pupils to refine their own questioning and consider more varied options. Open-ended tasks.

Pastoral work and cross-curricular issues
Connection between approaches taken in pastoral sessions and mathematics lessons. Mathematics as a tool for other subjects. Other subjects as a vehicle for using and applying mathematics.

On teaching practice I was rebuked for marking too leniently — 'they need to learn as quickly as possible that mathematics is very precise and to get top grades there must be no ambiguity whatsoever'.

In my first teaching post I started with a classroom which was rather small — a smallness which ensured that desks had to be arranged in pairs. After half a term I was moved to a bigger room. When I first went to examine it I found the desks arranged separately and was told 'you will find this much better as they won't be able to chat or copy each others' work'. There was a very strong unspoken message that said I was not to change this arrangement of furniture whatever my own preference or the protests from my pupils.

At least this situation helped him to see what were important aspects of his personal beliefs and the value of articulating them rather than simply acting them out. One task which may be of value to both student and mentor is to ask students to compare their experience of school as pupils with the school they find themselves in now, to identify similarities and differences, and hence to evaluate strengths and weaknesses.

We now examine through short case studies some of the possible points at which the personal beliefs and attitudes of the student — and the mentor — may be exposed in the process of evaluation. The quoted paragraphs contain the mentor's own account and interpretation of events. Our commentary pursues some aspects of this interpretation.

Mark

Mark had come near to failing on his first teaching practice which had been in a highly traditional school, because he had disliked imposing the constraints and sanctions which were customary in that setting. When his tutor suggested a school famous for its 'progressive' methods for his second practice he responded with enthusiasm, sure that he could show his true qualities as a teacher in that context. His mentor takes up the story.

Unfortunately he had interpreted the philosophy of 'responding to pupils' needs and interests' as meaning that he did not need to prepare for lessons, confident that his mathematical knowledge would carry him through. But without stimulus from him, interest was not forthcoming in the pupils. Furthermore the casual (though sincere) friendliness with which he approached them was seen by the teenage pupils as inappropriately overfamiliar, even intrusive and they resented it. Soon they began to play tricks on him. This distressed him greatly and led to a major clash between him and one of the more troubled pupils. It was only at this point that he was able to re-examine his initial assumptions and begin to work on being the teacher which with maturity he might become.

At this point Mark needed much supportive counselling and guidance in setting very strong parameters about how he would teach and interact with pupils. It was also important that the clash between him and the troubled pupil was explored and resolved. In the context of the school a very public handshake between the two of them was a crucial step in persuading the other pupils to give Mark space to try a different approach, though it was also necessary that his mentor should give intensive support while implementing his new learning.

Although there were still serious doubts and issues which needed to be raised in his final report the improvement he had shown was sufficient enough to allow him to pass. It was however a time of doubt and self-criticism for the mentor as well as for Mark. Should the crisis have been foreseen and perhaps averted or was it a necessary part of Mark's learning? With hindsight it seemed that Mark's major problem, manifested in both schools, was an immaturity which led him to seek easy popularity with the pupils. This is not an unusual phenomenon but nevertheless can be a difficult fact to point out.

It should be acknowledged that many mentors find it hard to play the role of critical friend when things are going wrong in a practice, but that this is a crucial aspect of the mentoring role. In Chapter 2 Peter Gates draws attention to the fine balance between challenge and support and the implications of this for mentoring.

Hema

Hema was another student who experienced some difficulties during her teaching practice but of quite a different nature to Mark. She was a mature student having raised a family and then completed an Open University course in mathematics. Her mentor describes Hema's attributes:

> She was committed, caring and thoughtful. Her expectations of herself were high and she tended to be very self-critical. Her preparation of lessons was good and her manner and approach with individual pupils was excellent. Her problems were with certain classes, who took advantage of her self-questioning approach which they perceived as weakness, and seized the opportunity to 'play up'. With younger pupils her classroom control was calm and effective. With less able groups of older pupils her caring attitude, patience and the time that she was prepared to devote to them, won her their affection. It was the older, more able students who caused her concern. When evaluating the situation herself, she was aware of the difficulties. Hema knew that she found it hard to be calm and assertive, at times, and that this was reflected in her voice.

For Hema evaluation by a mentor proved to be helpful. She needed someone to help her to focus on the many positive aspects of her teaching. She also needed help to realize that with more experience, together with her aware, reflective approach, she would eventually become clearer about her own aims. Her mentor's account continues:

> She needed to get a balance between questioning her practice in order to develop her skills and being decisive and definite enough to deal with less cooperative pupils. Without regular evaluation sessions Hema could quite easily have allowed her difficulties with one group to overshadow the successes that she had achieved with other groups that she was teaching. During the course of the practice she did realize that she had considerable strengths in certain areas. She became aware that she was successful in teaching less able pupils and that she particularly enjoyed this aspect of her work. She also realized that the groups of older pupils may have caused her less difficulty if she had taught them as younger pupils previously.
>
> In Hema's final assessment we both agreed that she had definite strengths and skills to offer as a teacher, that she had faced any difficulties openly and that her commitment would encourage her to continue to improve and develop as a teacher.

Often the most promising teachers will be the most self-critical as they will see more areas for development and improvement. Part of the mentor's job is providing a safe place for student-teachers to make their mistakes: 'You may never get it quite right with Class Y now, but you have learned from them and when you meet a similar situation in the future you will have some experience to draw on.'

The Mentor's Responsibilities in Evaluation

It is a narrow view of school-based teacher education to assume that learning to be a teacher and then learning to be a better teacher takes place *just* through experience of teaching. This book takes the position that experience alone is not enough for learning but that critical reflection on that experience is essential.* This necessarily implies that the student is being invited to engage in self-evaluation and assessment. It also implies that the mentor is a reflective practitioner as both teacher and mentor, and is also engaged in self-evaluation. In a climate of mutual trust both parties can learn from the other and use the other as observer in the process of supported self-evaluation. This was the case with Rosie and her mentor.

Rosie

Rosie had spent a year getting a master's degree in engineering in a very 'macho' setting, and as a result of this was very aware of gender issues in

---

* The theme of critical reflection is elaborated in Chapters 2, 5 and 10.

learning. She knew what she wanted to do as a teacher, for both the girls and the boys in her class. This soon led to a wider consideration of the role of social settings and customs in successful learning. With her the mentor was able to adopt a partnership approach.

> I taught several pairs of parallel classes. Rosie and I would share the planning for the introduction of a new topic, then one of us would present the initial lesson while the other observed. With the parallel class we swapped roles. This way we could look at the merits of our planning decisions as well as 'what was the same and what was different' about the responses of the two groups. Were differences a function of the groups themselves or were they traceable to differences in our own approaches?

Although both parties were clearly learning from the situation and enjoying it, there came a point where the mentor needed to stand back and assess whether the teaching tasks were the most appropriate in the circumstances. It was important to acknowledge that any task had three potential purposes: first to provide suitable learning experiences for the pupils, second to provide Rosie with appropriate experience of teaching and only third to contribute to the mentor's own development or convenience. Included in the mentor's self-evaluation must be consideration of whether this order of priorities has been achieved.

When things are going well, as with Rosie, the difficult aspect of evaluation is to recognize the questions. In a less happy situation the points for evaluation and judgment may be more obvious and also more painful. There are two important questions:

- Is my assessment of the student accurate — have I sufficient evidence for my opinions?
- Is my assessment of the student fair — or is my judgment being clouded by personal preferences in teaching or my relationship with the student?

If there are doubts about a student's overall suitability for teaching one strategy is to check out your impressions with other concerned people. Most obviously this will be other teachers in the school with whom the student has worked, especially a professional tutor, if there is one, and with the tutor in the HE Department. These were all involved in the discussions about Mark mentioned earlier. Sometimes, too, the viewpoint of pupils can be very relevant. The aims and motives of pupils are not themselves always easy to assess — it can be dangerous to take them at face value — but since they are in the classroom all of the time it is worth checking out their observations when these are offered. Consider the case of Rob as told by his mentor.

Rob

Rob was a student learning to teach PE as a main subject and mathematics as a second subject. He was tall and confident and he seemed to be having a successful teaching practice as far as his main subject was concerned. On the surface the mathematics classroom appeared orderly and the pupils seemed to be occupied with the tasks. Rob clearly felt that he was managing the situation well.

Regarding his teaching of mathematics, however, there was cause for concern.

As the usual class teacher I was inundated with requests for help from pupils, after lessons taken by Rob. The pupils offered various explanations for why they had not resolved their difficulties during the lessons. These included such responses as: not liking him, feeling that he did not explain things very well, worrying that they might be picked on. When questioned further the pupils offered few actual incidents that had led them to form their opinions of Rob, but they did seem genuinely anxious and fearful.

The pupils' responses gave a clue to Rob's limitations which the mentor was able to follow up.

In discussion with Rob it was clear that he was tending to underestimate the complexities of certain topics tackled and also the difficulties that his size and confident manner could contribute towards pupils fearing him. He had also not considered that teaching styles he had perceived as successful, as a pupil himself, may not be the most effective generally.

However lack of sensitivity can be a very difficult issue to explore and work on.

Having assessed a lack of awareness quite early in the practice, I needed to work out how to respond to this problem. My first response was to discuss the presentation of certain topics in more detail with Rob. I tried to encourage him to question and explore strategies and approaches that might lead pupils towards feeling successful and confident about their learning. I also suggested ways in which he could assess in more depth pupils' understanding of tasks tackled.

Although Rob was prepared to discuss issues up to a point, he seemed unconvinced of the need to check his own assumptions about the pupils' learning. He disagreed with some of the teaching styles he had observed in the school and thought we were asking him to devote too much time to what was his second subject.

The next step was to involve the tutor from the HE Department.

> In addition to discussion with Rob and my own observations, I also discussed the issues of awareness and relationships with pupils with Rob's tutor from the university. We both attempted to focus Rob's attention on these issues, and as a result he agreed that improvements in these directions were desirable, but in fact little change resulted. It was a short practice and, without total commitment from Rob, I did not feel that I had observed enough indications that Rob would work towards improving his teaching of mathematics in a thoughtful and understanding way. At the end of the teaching practice, with agreement from the tutor, my assessment had to be that Rob still needed to look at issues relating to the teaching of mathematics in greater depth. He needed to assess his own commitment towards this subject and tackle a further teaching practice in a more questioning and sensitive way.

Here is a situation in which the mentor has observed problems but has not been given any indication by the student that those problems would be resolved. She is aware that she is not assessing absolute achievement, but progress towards being a better teacher and a willingness to go on learning. The lack of progress and commitment were perhaps the most important indicators of an unsuccessful practice in this case.

> The discussion of my final assessment with Rob was not ideal. Usually I find a great deal of agreement between a student and myself about the issues raised. Although Rob may have felt that my expectations were rather high of a 'part-time' mathematics teacher, I needed to consider the needs of pupils who might in future experience him as their 'full-time' mathematics teacher. Rob may still not agree with my assessment. Our order of priorities certainly differed, but I do feel that it would have been more difficult for him to accept the emphases in my final report if issues had not been raised in a positive way and discussed throughout the practice between Rob, myself and his tutor.

Rob's final report may not have been as he might personally have hoped but its content was not unexpected or unexplained.

Extreme Cases

Sometimes the mentor has the unpleasant task of being the person to say a student-teacher is failing. This should be very infrequent if the appropriate ongoing evaluation has been carried out — in most cases genuinely unsuitable students will withdraw of their own accord or on advice from their mentor and tutor, as was the case with Jenny.

Jenny

Jenny had had a very successful university career and had gained an excellent degree in mathematics. She was quite shocked to discover that, not only did few of the pupils appear to share her enthusiasm for the subject, but that many of them found her to be a source of amusement. She found it very hard to relate to the youngsters and soon decided that teaching — at least at school — was not for her. The mentor — and tutor — still had a role in supporting and counselling her as she made that decision and began to look for alternatives.

This case study yet again highlights the importance of early discussion of problems that arise. In this instance it was necessary to disentangle indications of possible failure from those issues which could be worked on in a positive way.

In other cases the mentor may feel the student would actually be damaging or dangerous as a teacher and the grounds for this may need to be clearly spelled out to all concerned. Where this involves a reckless disregard for the safety of pupils the manifestations may be very obvious, but psychological dangers may be harder to pin-point. John's mentor was faced with this problem.

John

John was an able mathematician who seemed to have an obsession with 'winning', with scoring points and being acknowledged as the cleverest person present. This was annoying for the staff but sometimes very upsetting for the pupils. His mentor saw that some pupils were being continually undermined by him through no fault of their own, and was worried about the cumulative damage this could cause. He had the unpleasant but entirely necessary task of making this tendency explicit to the student and in the final report, backing his judgment that John did not have the personal skills to become a teacher.

Fortunately such situations are quite rare and will never be faced alone as the decision to fail a student will be shared between the school and the HE Department through negotiation with all those involved in the mentoring and tutoring processes. Also they can to some extent be balanced against the pleasant task of being the person to recommend a very good student for a distinction.

Summary

Evaluation is an integral part of the mentoring process and has an important role to play in achieving the aims and objectives of the practice.

One specific objective is to encourage self-evaluation and a reflective self-evaluative mentor can be a powerful role model for the student-teacher.

Mentor and student can both learn about their personal values and feelings about assessment through engagement in evaluation and assessment of teaching.

The mentor also has a responsibility to evaluate the experience offered to the student-teacher. This must be done bearing in mind the needs of the pupils in the school and the mentor's responsibilities as a teacher. Sometimes it is necessary to declare priorities if student and pupil needs seem to be in conflict.

Planning, preparation and sharing information all contribute to an effective evaluative partnership between student, mentor and tutor.

In most cases, through the process of evaluation, including their final assessment, mentors help students develop their potential and become more effective practitioners, and this is experienced positively by both parties. Nevertheless, sometimes the mentor has to take on a judgmental role and must be prepared to give a realistic appraisal even when this is critical or unwelcome.

Chapter 10

Mentoring, Co-mentoring, and the Inner Mentor

Barbara Jaworski and Anne Watson

In what ways can mentoring go beyond working with student teachers, perhaps to influence the development of mathematics teaching and to improve the learning experiences for pupils in mathematics classrooms more widely? This chapter suggests that mentoring extends naturally to collaborative activity with colleagues, and to enquiry into our own practice as teachers.

Where Do We Go Next?

Many readers will recognize feelings of apprehension and inadequacy which often accompany people when starting a new job. In the early days, one's focus may be to get through the practicalities of the day, to keep relatively up-to-date, and to know where to get help. After a while, one hopes, a second phase occurs in which there is time to think about the work in a broader sense — to develop the basics, introduce small innovations, explore links with other people. Perhaps there is a deeper understanding of how the job fits the whole picture and one might search for ways to adapt it to fit one's own needs and interests as well as those of the institution.

New mentors may be concerned with knowing the course, timetabling the students, keeping their own teaching going, establishing contact with the HE Department, and so on. In this chapter we suggest other possible aspects of mentoring which might be developed by an experienced mentor or by a mathematics department. Some of these may be seen as leading to the professional development of the *mentor*, but many more are about developing the process of *mentoring* as part of the work of other teachers or the whole mathematics department.

Figure 10.1 illustrates and contrasts possible ways in which mentoring may grow in a department. The central relationship is that of the mentor and

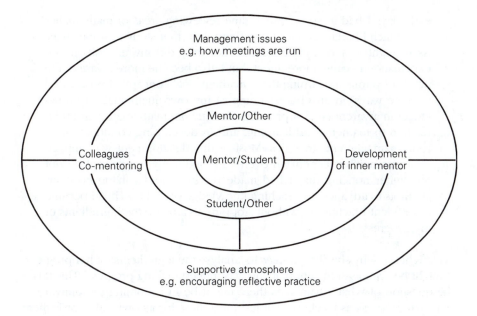

Figure 10.1

student. From this the mentor and the student may develop similar relationships with other teachers and students. Other colleagues may begin to act as mentors for each other or may find they are beginning to develop their awareness of their own teaching, operating as a kind of *inner mentor*. The structure and atmosphere of the department can enable and encourage the growth of these roles through sensitive management. The rest of this book has been about the central relationship. We will now explore those other possibilities.

Becoming More Aware of How We Teach, and *Why*

A teacher education course can be seen as a time and place to start the process of developing mathematics teaching. Earlier chapters have looked at many aspects of this process, and raised essential issues. The process of development does not stop when a student-teacher gets a teaching job. Some teaching approaches and strategies develop naturally during the practice of teaching. Changes occur. Any experienced teacher is a *different* teacher to the one who first began. Many teachers, when motivated to look back on their own practice, discover that their development has been largely unconscious. One teacher that we talked to wrote about her practice as follows:

> I know that as I became more confident within the classroom, and more aware of what I wanted to achieve, I became a more competent practitioner. My own mathematical knowledge also developed. In my

early days I had to spend much time reviewing areas of mathematics with which I had lost contact. I undertook further study in some areas. As I taught lessons in these areas, not only did my exposition and explanation became more fluent, but I also became more aware of the needs of pupils in learning these mathematical concepts. I progressed in three ways: in an understanding of my own mathematical knowledge; in awareness of approaches to *teaching* mathematics and their relation to mathematical learning; and in developing confident classroom management strategies. Most of this development was implicit — it was neither recognized overtly nor explicitly triggered. I do not remember noticing that I had made progress, and I made no overt attempts to advance my teaching knowledge or ability. Thus I became a confident practitioner without stopping to analyse the ingredients of my progress.

We might ask why she should *need* to 'analyse the ingredients' of her progress. It might be seen as sufficient that she was indeed making progress. This raises the question of what advantages there might be in becoming more aware of our own progress as teachers. Is it just awareness for its own sake, or is there some value in terms of benefits for the pupils we teach?

At a recent meeting of mathematics mentors in Oxford, one mentor said the following:

> One thing which I've found valuable, once I got over the initial feeling of being threatened by it, is that when a student-teacher asks me why I do something, I have to try to explain something which I've never really thought about before. I have to ask myself, 'why *do* I do that?' And struggling to answer the question makes me learn something about myself which can make me a more effective teacher.

As Stephanie Prestage and Pat Perks point out in Chapter 6, recognition of 'this is where I was' and 'this is where I now am' and asking 'why and how have I changed?' leads to greater self-awareness. Knowing more about yourself can reinforce something you feel good about. It can also offer the possibility of change — if that is appropriate. Perhaps purposeful change is more *possible* when there is awareness. One of the most important consequences of the *mentoring* process might be seen as the knowledge which mentors develop of their own practice through working with student-teachers.

Perhaps in order to be a better mentor I have to 'know myself'. An understanding of how I can help someone else to change or develop must be enhanced by an awareness of how I myself have changed. To go even further, perhaps the more I act to become aware of and to work on my own practice, the more insight I can gain into the mentoring process and become a more effective mentor. I might simultaneously become a better teacher.

One of the benefits for the student-teacher of a mentoring approach to

learning to teach is the availability of another person to act as a *critical friend.**
When the student-teacher becomes a fully-fledged teacher, this need for a
critical friend does not go away, although there is likely to be no designated
person to fulfil the role. The more experienced one becomes, the less need is
perceived for such a critical friend. Yet, however experienced a teacher is, a
critical friend is still a powerful force in the development of teaching. This was
supported by an experience reported by a colleague who had been doing
research with two teachers in their classrooms:

> I worked with two mathematics teachers in the same school, where
> we engaged jointly in some classroom research. On one day each
> week, we each taught lessons, which we had planned jointly, and
> observed each other's teaching. At the end of a day of working to-
> gether we sat down for an hour to talk over the experiences of the day
> and recorded our conversation on audio tape. Afterwards, I replayed
> the tape, listening to our conversation and making a note of aspects
> of it which were significant for me. I wrote down some of my thoughts,
> and posted this off to the teachers so that they would receive it before
> our next meeting.
>
> Both of them said to me, jointly and separately, that our work
> together was valuable for them because it encouraged them to think
> about their teaching in a way that they might not otherwise have
> done. They found the joint planning of value because talking over
> ideas for a lesson helped to crystallize objectives, and three heads
> were better than one in devising activities. They found the end-of-day
> reflection of value, because it provided the opportunity to compare
> experiences and share concerns with two others who were closely
> acquainted with what was involved. They were happy to comment on
> my written accounts because these related directly to our joint work
> and to issues with which they were directly concerned. When our
> work came to an end, they said with determination that they would
> continue to work together in much the way we had as a threesome.
>
> When I talked with them again, some time later, they said, with
> regret, that they had not continued to work together as they had
> suggested. Pressures of normal school life had taken priority.

One interpretation of what occurred is that what was of most value for the
teachers here was the role the researcher played of 'critical friend'. It is possible that they were unable to fulfil the role of critical friend for each other.

There is a difficulty in initiating and maintaining a relationship of critical
friend — 'critical friendship' — in a school. The pressures on a teacher's time
militate against giving the time such a relationship requires. It may be easier
to create time when there is a formal relationship. Perhaps finding time for
collaboration between colleagues can happen more readily when there is a

* This term has been discussed previously in Chapters 1 and 4.

defined task of sufficient immediacy to promote it to the top of a list of priorities.

However, the relationship requires more than just time. It needs a commitment to development through which it is possible to invest energy and cope with uncertainty. It is potentially threatening in its demands on personal involvement. All of this raises questions about how such relationships begin and what is necessary to sustain them.

A critical friendship is potentially different between colleagues than between mentor and student due to a mutuality which the mentor–student relationship lacks. As well as a degree of trust and confidence between those involved, this may be dependent on some equality of power within the relationship. Teachers can choose their friends more freely than students their mentors.

The mentor–student relationship (as well as to some extent that of researcher–teacher expressed in the anecdote) has one advantage, however. There is one member of the partnership who has *responsibility* to initiate discussions and the raising of issues. This person is able where appropriate to take on a leadership role. In a working critical friendship, colleagues would be likely to share this responsibility, each feeling free to start a conversation with a casual question or comment or a more deliberate invitation to discussion. However, a barrier to the development of a critical friendship might be the inability of either teacher to initiate professional conversation, perhaps through lack of confidence in raising issues or of awareness of issues on which to work. It may be that what is needed is opportunity to work together in a non-threatening way first in order to develop trust and confidence, and to become aware of issues of mutual concern.

A value we ourselves gain from colleagues who act as critical friends is that they ask questions about what we do and why we do it, and encourage critical reflection. Some of the questions are hard to answer. They require hard thinking, and there are not obvious or easy-to-find answers. The following excerpt from a conversation provides an example of questions which can prove difficult to answer.

The teacher had planned an activity designed to address National Curriculum Attainment Targets concerning 'surface area':

Teacher: If today's activity doesn't get them there, I will try and develop a different activity that *will* get them there

Questioner: What does 'getting them there' look like, and how will you recognize it?

Teacher: [Wryly] All I can say is I wish you wouldn't ask such difficult questions!!!

Despite the difficulty, the question led to some valuable discussion on what was involved in pupils grasping a given mathematical concept — in this case, surface area — and a teacher's recognition of what had been learned.

Addressing such 'difficult questions' can be very valuable for a teacher in terms of personal learning. Student-teachers may ask hard questions without considering their implication. They simply want to know. (For example, 'How do you get them to remember what you taught them last week?') It is probably harder for experienced practitioners to ask the questions, perhaps because they *know* they are hard questions, perhaps because of an implied sense of inadequacy in not knowing the answers.

The next section addresses some of these issues by looking at what is possible when colleagues within a department collaborate, both in the mentoring process with student teachers and in other activities related to teaching and learning mathematics, thereby creating an environment through which critical friendships can develop.

Co-mentoring

Our experience of working with other mentors suggests that the skills they develop by working with students become part of their practice in a wider sense. As a result they may become more reflective about their own work. This leads to a greater awareness of their practice, through which they are likely to have sympathy and understanding for others, and may also be responsible for initiating reflection in others. Mentors who are used to acting as critical friend will be aware of many issues facing teachers, and acting as supportive colleagues is a natural extension of their work with student-teachers. A mentor can also act as a stimulus within a mathematics department, raising awareness of issues and helping to create an effective team.

In some schools one teacher may have responsibility for professional development of new staff, or even the whole staff, under a title such as 'professional tutor', or 'director of studies', and may take the role of INSET leader, organizing activities on in-service days. What we are suggesting here is that professional development might also happen on a more personal basis building on the ideas of mentoring presented in this book. It is possible to approach professional relationships between teachers from the point of view of *mentoring each other*, taking responsibility for each other's development as well as one's own, which we shall call *co-mentoring*. The idea of co-mentoring can underpin all work which teachers do together whether in pairs or in larger groups. The work might arise from an external agenda, a whole school's agenda, or the department's own agenda. Here are some examples of school activities which may be approached from a co-mentoring perspective, or which create an atmosphere in which co-mentoring can develop.

External Agendas

Staff appraisal
Many recognized appraisal schemes are based on an initial discussion between appraiser and appraisee in which the focus of appraisal is identified. Information

is collected from contributors chosen by the appraisee. The appraiser observes lessons with the agreed focus in mind and the observations and contributions are discussed. Plans for future development arise from this discussion. In such a scheme the appraiser is behaving as a mentor.

Changes in syllabus

In 1988 the introduction of GCSE meant that all departments had to change their syllabus, and this happened again in preparation for the Key Stage 4 assessment of the National Curriculum in 1994. Rather than being treated as an administrative exercise, this can alternatively be seen as an opportunity for teachers within the department to review aims and objectives, to reflect on practice and to set targets for the future. They can support each other in reaching targets and evaluating progress, in pairs or otherwise. Through this it is likely that a joint sense of purpose grows and a common philosophy is strengthened.

Teacher assessment

In coming to terms with assessment demands related to the National Curriculum, teachers have found themselves using statements of attainment to trigger discussions about what they believed mathematics to be and how they might become better at getting pupils to think and act mathematically.* In early 1992 most secondary teachers in England and Wales explored an activity called 'octagon loops' in order to prepare themselves for the pilot SATs. In many cases they found themselves, possibly for the first time, doing mathematics with other teachers and rediscovering what it feels like to learn together.

Shared Agendas

Every school has other groups or institutions with which it works, for example, parents, employers, feeder schools, HE Departments and so on. It may be possible to work with them in a co-mentoring style.

An example of this, which has been called, sometimes confusingly, IT INSET (standing for *I*nitial *T*eacher Education and *I*nse*r*vice Education for *T*eachers jointly, and nothing to do with Information Technology), has involved cooperative work between student-teachers and their tutors from an HE Department and teachers and pupils in a school.† This recognizes that these groups have much to learn from each other. A particular example involved the use of television in the classroom. An HE tutor wanted to try out a particular television programme with a class of pupils. The head of mathematics in the school asked that the event could be used for INSET for the

---

* The integration of AT1 with work addressing other Attainment Targets, as discussed in Chapter 7, could be a basis for valuable discussion.
† IT INSET was pioneered by a group in Leicestershire whose work is described in Ashton *et al.* (1983).

mathematics team. The tutor felt that this offered a good opportunity also to involve student-teachers. In the event a group of students, two tutors and several teachers worked with a number of Year 8 classes and the same television programme. They all met afterwards to debrief what had occurred and discuss issues arising from it. The discussion was considered to be so valuable that future meetings were organized in a similar style.

Whole School Agenda

Displays

The creation of a mathematics display for a parents' evening or some other event can be an opportunity for development if it starts with some questions like 'What do we want to say about mathematics or about our teaching?' and 'How does my pupils' work reflect this?', 'What needs to be said to pupils, parents, colleagues about this?'. In asking these questions teachers will share some of their own perceptions of mathematics and consider the effectiveness of their teaching. There was significant discussion of this in Chapter 3.

INSET days

Sometimes a topic is set for the whole school and departments are left to decide on the way in which they will approach it. One school had a language day during which the mathematics department looked at excerpts from mathematics books, media, a passage from a novel involving a conversation about mathematics, and some racing statistics. Together teachers in the department grappled with interpreting these sources and came to some general aims. The first was about limiting their use of the printed material to what was clear and accessible. The second was to become more aware of their own use of language in the classroom. The shared decision enabled them all to feel supported in their attempts to change.

School issues

Some schools ask all departments to consider various issues from time to time. In planning a discussion on underachievement one head of department asked members of her team each to prepare an anecdote about how they encouraged underachieving pupils. The result of sharing these anecdotes was that good practice was acknowledged and shared, no one felt they were being criticized, and all present felt able to admit that this was an aspect of their work which they could improve.

Mutual Support and Observation

A scheme, known as Mutual Support and Observation (MSO), exists in some schools where teachers from different disciplines pair up to observe, discuss and learn from each other's work. Peter Gates (1989) discusses one such scheme in which a mathematics teacher and an English teacher worked together over a period of time. The partnership contributed strongly to their professional development. This is just one way in which mathematics teachers can share with and learn from those in other disciplines. More informal arrangements between teachers in different subject areas could lead to sharing of ideas. Barrie Galpin and Simon Haines discuss this further in exploring cross-curricular issues in Chapter 8.

Departmental Agenda

Structure of meetings

If administrative matters are dealt with on paper, the departmental meeting can become a forum to discuss ways to improve the teaching and learning of mathematics within the school. Good quality discussions can be planned by:

- rotating the chair (!);
- having an agenda to which all can contribute;
- allowing time for people to prepare for the meeting by producing papers in advance;
- asking some people to prepare inputs to the meeting;
- starting, or finishing, by enabling everyone to speak once without interruption;
- ensuring that there is a clear outcome.

If all teachers have an input, they may feel more able to participate in change for themselves and others. Reflection on any proposed action can be arranged at some future date.

Discussion of pupils' work

Teachers can share informally their experiences of a particular activity or approach, but the atmosphere which allows this has to be nurtured. For example, in one school, all Year 10 classes had done some investigative work based on a common starting point prepared by one member of the department. Teachers met to discuss judgments which each teacher had made in marking the work. There were several different interpretations of both the marking scheme and the mathematics involved. It became clear that the differences lay in what each teacher valued, and it was this which influenced their judgments. The need for a shared outcome, in terms of consistency of marking pupils' work, meant that the overt tackling of differences became a joint activity. This was instrumental in creating an atmosphere conducive to sharing, and paved the way for other differences to be aired openly in the future.

Working with video excerpts

Classroom videotape can be a powerful catalyst for co-mentoring. At one of their houses, over an evening pizza and glass of wine, several teachers gathered to watch a video made during a mathematics lesson at their school. The discussion started with the filmed teacher giving his account of the lesson and the episode shown. The atmosphere was congenial enough to reduce his vulnerability. The group had agreed to be kind and positive, although probing in their comments and questions in order to get at issues of importance to them all. In this case a debate ensued about the 'pros and cons' of introducing work in an open-ended way or a more directed way. Some of the teachers resolved to try different types of approach in future as a result of seeing their colleague in action.

Mentoring role
It is likely that any student-teacher in a school works with many of the teachers in the department, and that some discussion of the programme and its aims for the student-teachers would be valuable. This could lead to collaborative work which might also involve student teachers. The mentor could act as an unofficial group leader, facilitating discussion, although not directing its content.*

Tapping into students' knowledge
There is an interesting side-effect of sharing the mentoring throughout the department. The student works with a variety of styles, hears a variety of comments, absorbs a variety of ideas and may end up being the one person in the department who has the fullest idea of what is going on and how the total philosophy works in practice. The rest of the team can valuably tap into this knowledge.

In all of the situations described briefly above, there are opportunities to encourage, question and praise, to look for things to celebrate, to help set targets, to notice unspoken concerns and to help each other reflect. Such opportunities can be described broadly as *co-mentoring*. Creating or grasping these opportunities leads to the development of an atmosphere through which teachers' awareness of issues of importance in their teaching grows, and through which professional development takes place naturally.

Reflective Practice — The Inner Mentor

Reflection and Action

Many of the earlier chapters have referred to the value of reflection. In Chapter 5 Stephen Lerman talked of Donald Schön's (1987) concept of reflection-in-action. In Chapter 6, Pat Perks and Stephanie Prestage emphasized the

---

* The Mathematical Association document *Develop your Teaching* (1991) addresses the role of group leader explicitly alongside case studies of teachers who have worked together to further their professional development, and a way of working is described which can be used as a basis for exploring issues in the teaching and learning of mathematics.

importance of evaluation, which involves reflection. Inevitably, for different people, a term like 'reflection' will have slightly different usages or interpretations. Our preferred view of the term is one which overtly recognizes an element of action resulting from considered thought. John Dewey (1933) spoke of *reflective thinking* as follows:

> *Reflective* thinking, in distinction to other operations to which we apply the name of thought, involves (1) a state of doubt, hesitation, mental difficulty, in which thinking originates, and (2) an act of searching, hunting, enquiring, to find material that will resolve the doubt, settle and dispose of the complexity. (p. 12)

Thus reflection becomes a combination of thought and action through which what is problematic is identified and tackled. Schön's 'reflection-in-action' is consistent with this, and evaluation usually leads to plans for future action.

In the last section we spoke of co-mentoring, which involves talking together about aspects of teaching and learning mathematics, and crucially about asking questions of each other which force awareness of issues of concern. These can be personal to any individual teacher or can relate to wider agendas. Such forcing of awareness creates a reflective situation from which some form of action results. This might be a *considered* action, in that a teacher decides to *do* something — like approach a mathematical topic in a new way, or use a different classroom management technique, or watch out for instances of closed questioning. It might be an action which manifests itself in on-the-spot decision-making which is influenced by forced awareness in some situation.

Teachers who have become more aware of their own practice, perhaps through mentoring or co-mentoring, might be in a position to make the act of reflecting a more self-conscious one We have found that the following sequence (or cycle) of stages can occur in reflective practice.*

1 *Noticing significant events*
   This might arise from a forcing of awareness, perhaps by a question asked by a colleague. It might be a critical incident which arises during a lesson. It may be something we read in a book which triggers awareness.

2 *Giving an account of the event*
   This involves articulating what was involved. It may involve describing to someone else. It may be a time to replay what occurred for our own benefit. It may involve writing a brief but vivid account in a journal. In any case it is a stage of trying simply to say what was involved without overt interpretation.

---

* Chapter 2 offers a similar cycle which you may like to compare. See also Mathematical Association (1991).

3   *Critical analysis of the event*
    This involves asking questions about our *reasons* for finding the event
    significant, trying to analyze what was important about it, trying to
    account *for* the interpretations we find ourselves making. The word
    critical implies that there is some *critiquing* involved, some deliberate
    attempt to reach for essential issues.

4. *Consequent action*
    This involves *doing* something as a result of our thinking and analysis.
    It may be that we wish to initiate some form of action as a direct result
    of our thinking. It may be that our thinking has led to our being aware
    of some issue so that we are more ready to notice instances of it when
    they occur.

Although the above process might appear linear, it is more likely in practice
to be cyclic with the stages folding back on themselves as further events take
place. All of these stages can occur through our talking with and working
alongside a colleague or student-teacher, but they do not *need* other involvement. Perhaps the most powerful capacity which one can develop as a
result of mentoring and co-mentoring, is how to be a mentor for oneself. We
would like to refer to this as the 'inner mentor'.

The Inner Mentor

One develops an inner mentor when the process of reflection and action
becomes unselfconscious, and occurs naturally as a part of day-to-day practice. Thus we find ourselves recognizing critical incidents, analyzing them, and
taking action almost automatically. We would like to illustrate this by providing an example from our own practice.

One of us read a book about drama teaching, in which the author talked
about taking on the 'mantle of the expert'.* This triggered a reaction of 'yes,
I could use that', and subsequently of 'I *do* use that'. It created an awareness
of situations in the classroom where it is valuable for pupils to 'take on the
mantle of the expert', for example, when a pupil has worked on some
mathematical idea and is asked to express this for someone else. In this situation the pupil *is* the expert. No one else can express that idea, or explain that
thinking. If the teacher says, 'you're the expert', this at once values the pupil's
thinking, and provides a confidence boost. On the other hand, a pupil could
be *asked* to be the expert — to act 'as if' they had expertise in some situation
— perhaps to come up to the front of the classroom and explain the theorem
of Pythagoras 'as if you were Pythagoras' — '*be* the expert'. Pretending you're
an expert can be an act which encourages you to be more actively and con-
fidently involved in the thinking. It is likely now that some situation will arise,

---

* For disussion of the idea of 'mantle of the expert' see Johnson and O'Neill (1984).

when we are in the classroom, in which we will find it quite natural to ask a pupil to 'be the expert'.

It is possible to go further than this. Having noticed something like the 'mantle of the expert' it would be possible to carry out some personal project to investigate its effectiveness. This might be done by deciding (say, in lessons with Year 9 for the next month) to instigate a new technique of inviting pupils to 'be an expert', and deliberately to observe what happens when the technique is used. It may be that different effects occur in recognizably different situations. It may be that what occurs on some occasion is surprising, and that this can be checked against other instances. It may be that as pupils get used to being asked to 'be the expert', they offer themselves to take on the role without the teacher having to mention it. As a result of experimentation and observation, a picture is likely to emerge of the value of the technique and its effects and implications. It may be valuable to share this with colleagues, or write an article for other teachers to read in an educational journal.*

What this example has described is a form of 'action research'. It consists of deliberate action taken as a result of personal reflection in order to investigate some way of developing the teaching of mathematics. It is designed to improve, ultimately, the experience of pupils in their learning of mathematics. In all the talk about mentoring and reflection it is possible to lose sight of this main aim in developing teaching, that is, to improve the learning experiences of pupils.[†]

As teachers, we have been aware of research by other people in the area of mathematics education which has been of value to our teaching, but recognize that much research has no impact on the actual teaching of mathematics in the classroom. Part of the problem is dissemination, but part is also its perceived relevance or lack of relevance to a teacher's own situation. This may make it difficult to turn reflection on such research into action. However, if teachers conduct research themselves, it not only has immediate impact in terms of classroom effects, and individual teacher development, it has a credibility which is intrinsic in its direct link to practice.

Developing an inner mentor opens up the possibility of undertaking one's own research. This need not be formidable or excessively time consuming. At the very simplest level it involves classroom enquiry — trying out ideas, noticing what happens, and reflecting on experiences in our own classrooms.

A secondary effect might be what others can learn when we communicate what *we* learn, either by word of mouth to our colleagues or through some published account. However, a project at York University, in which a group of teachers engaged in action research as part of a funded higher degree project had an interesting outcome according to Vulliamy and Webb (1991). They reported that LEA advisors who evaluated the project placed more value

---

* For example Mathematical Association's 'Mathematics in School', or ATM's 'Mathematics Teaching'.
[†] Further examples of action research undertaken by teachers of mathematics may be found in the ATM publication *Teacher as Researcher*, ATM (1987).

on the effect which systematic enquiry had on the quality of the teaching with which it was associated than on any dissemination of outcomes of the research. It is thus a worthwhile objective to do such research purely for our own benefit and not to be put off by a need to record and publish results.

Another advantageous effect might be that such research feeds back into the institution concerned, perhaps in influencing fellow practitioners, either indirectly, or directly through co-mentoring. An example of this occurred when three young teachers in a school were each given an incentive allowance for contributing to small-scale action research within the school. The effect of this was to give them confidence to approach colleagues to ask questions and to talk about aspects of teaching. As a result of the debate which followed, other teachers within the school became involved in thinking about and changing classroom practice.

The Development of Mathematics Teaching

This book has, at length, suggested ways of developing reflective practice both during and after one's time as a student teacher. It has offered ways in which mentoring, co-mentoring and inner-mentoring may be structured and sustained.

Reflective practice frequently leads to self-development and increased self-knowledge. Mentors often comment that they have to be prepared to unpack their own work in order to do a good job with their students. By 'unpack' we mean to take one's practice apart, lay it out and look at the constituent parts afresh, maybe seeing how they fit together or even putting them together a different way. It can be an uncomfortable process to look closely at your own teaching, and therefore needs to be justified as worthwhile. How can reflection *guarantee* that the teaching of children and the teaching of mathematics will improve as a result?

First, reflection is about what happens in the classroom. It may be inspired by something outside school, such as a passage in a book, a conversation, or the actions of others. It may be sparked off by something *in* school, such as a comment from a pupil, a surprising examination result, or watching a colleague at work. In either case, what is being used as raw material comes *from* the classroom.

Second, reflection should avoid becoming fanciful, divorced from the classroom. The critical analysis stage of the cycle described in the last section should ensure that the structure in which the reflective process takes place provides a reference point. Keeping reflection firmly linked to classroom issues is quite difficult to do just in your own head. Regular meetings with a colleague or colleagues, or the keeping of a personal diary whose function is to record and remind, could help to keep one's feet on the ground. In 'reflective practice', the emphasis should be on the 'practice', as much as on the 'reflective'. It is important to turn reflections into actions.

It is these actions which affect pupils in the classroom. If we have *thought* about how children learn mathematics, and how our teaching influences this learning, then the next stage must be to develop strategies which enable us to put our thinking into practice. Such strategies may involve ways of saying, acting, asking and being in the classroom. If they are successful this implies that the learning environment for pupils is improved. By monitoring the strategies, and continuing to use those which seem successful it is likely that they become automatic aspects of day-to-day practice. Perhaps one day it would be hard to recall how they initially developed.

Lastly it is important to be aware overtly of parallels between our own learning as teachers and ways in which our *pupils* learn. The opening chapter emphasized how mentoring can be like teaching. One of our aims as mentors is to enable teachers to be reflective practitioners in the future so that they can adapt as the demands on them grow and change. Moreover, as teachers we could try to pass on the valuable skills of reflective learning to our *pupils* in order to feel that we have to some degree equipped them for the unknown intellectual and social challenges that lie ahead. We can only do this effectively if we fully understand those skills ourselves.

References

ASHTON, P.M.E. *et al.* (1983) *Teacher Education in the Classroom: Initial and Inservice,* London, Croom Helm.

ASSOCIATION OF TEACHERS OF MATHEMATICS (1987) *Teacher as Researcher,* Derby, ATM.

DEWEY J. (1933) *How We Think,* London, D.C. Heath and Company.

GATES, P. (1989) 'Developing conscious and pedagogical knowledge through mutual observation' in WOODS, P. (Ed.) *Working for Teacher Development,* London, Peter Francis.

JOHNSON, L. and O'NEILL, C. (Eds) (1984) *Dorothy Heathcote: Collected Writings on Education and Drama,* Cheltenham, Stanley Thornes.

MATHEMATICAL ASSOCIATION (1991) *Develop your Teaching,* Cheltenham, Stanley Thornes.

SCHÖN, D. (1987) *Educating the Reflective Practitioner,* Oxford, Jossey-Bass.

VULLIAMY G. and WEBB, R. (1991) 'Teacher research and educational change', *British Educational Research Journal,* **17**, 3, pp. 219–36.

Notes on Contributors

Maggie Crosson has been a teacher of mathematics for fourteen years. She worked at Leysland High School in Countesthorpe, Leicestershire, where she undertook a variety of projects and tutoring roles with student-teachers from Leicester University. She has also worked with student teachers from Loughborough University and she is at present head of the mathematics department at Ibstock Community College.

Doug French is a lecturer in the School of Education at the University of Hull. He was formerly head of the mathematics department at Beacon School, a comprehensive school at Crowborough in East Sussex, where he also acted as a teacher–tutor for the school-based PGCE course run by the University of Sussex.

Barrie Galpin taught for thirteen years in comprehensive schools in Cambridgeshire, latterly as head of department. Following a period of work at Leicester University where he engaged in research and initial teacher education, he moved to the Centre for Mathematics Education at the Open University. His present work includes the production and promotion of materials to support the professional development of teachers of mathematics.

Peter Gates was formerly a mathematics teacher for thirteen years, latterly as head of mathematics at Stantonbury Campus in Milton Keynes. After this he worked as a lecturer in mathematics education at the Open University and at Bath University where he was responsible for the mathematics education component of the PGCE programme and was also involved in mentor training. He currently works in the School of Education at the University of Nottingham.

Simon Haines is currently hall curriculum leader in mathematics at Stantonbury Campus, Milton Keynes, and previously worked at Peers School, Oxford. He has been a mentor at both schools, and has worked as an occasional tutor at Southampton and Oxford Universities.

Barbara Jaworski is a lecturer at the University of Oxford Department of Educational Studies, and works with PGCE students in the Oxfordshire internship scheme. She was formerly a mathematics teacher, head of mathematics and lecturer in mathematics education at the Open University and at the University of Birmingham.

Stephen Lerman taught mathematics in secondary schools in Britain and Israel, and was head of mathematics in a London comprehensive school for five years. He is currently senior lecturer at the Centre for Mathematics Education, South Bank University, London. He teaches on initial and in-service courses, and also supervises research students.

Jean Melrose is a lecturer in the education department at Loughborough University. She works with, and claims to be learning continually from, pupils in secondary and primary schools, students preparing to be mathematics teachers, teachers in local schools and colleagues. She helped to complete Chapter 4, originally the work of Stephanie and Rita, after Rita's sudden death.

Rita Nolder was a lecturer in the education department at Loughborough University and worked closely with student-teachers and mentors. She was previously a mathematics teacher, and a mathematics advisory teacher in the Buckinghamshire mathematics support team. She died suddenly on 6 November 1992.

Pat Perks has been involved in mathematics education in Birmingham for many years — as mathematics teacher, head of department and as advisory teacher. She is currently a lecturer at the School of Education at the University of Birmingham.

Stephanie Prestage taught mathematics in London and was head of mathematics in a London comprehensive school. She is currently a lecturer in the School of Education at the University of Birmingham.

Susan E. Sanders is lecturer in mathematical education at the University College of Swansea. She is also director of the Post Graduate Certificate of Education (Primary) course. Previously she was senior advisory teacher for Mathematics for the City of Birmingham.

Christine Shiu has been a mathematics teacher in secondary schools in London and Leicestershire and a researcher at the Shell Centre for Mathematics Education at the University of Nottingham. In both of these roles she worked with students on PGCE courses. She now a senior lecturer at the Centre for Mathematics Education at the Open University, where she has worked on the production of distance-learning courses for teachers of mathematics.

Stephanie Smith is a mathematics teacher in a Leicestershire High School (11–14). She has responsibility for all student teachers coming into the school and liaising with tutors from HE Departments of education. She is an associate tutor at Leicester University School of Education.

Anne Watson was coordinator of mathematics at Peers School, Oxford, and has been associated with the internship scheme of the University of Oxford Department of Educational Studies for six years both as a mentor, head of department and in various other roles. She has recently taken up a post as senior lecturer in mathematics education at Nene College, Northampton.

Index

action: considered 134
   see also reflection-in-action
action research 63–4, 136–7
action researcher 63–4
activities, class: computer software for
   94
   transition between 86
advice: to student-teacher 8–9
   on teaching techniques 9
analysis: of critical incidents 53
analytical focus: on teaching 22
anecdotes: role of, and critical incidents
   53
apprehension: of student-teachers 124
approachability: of mentor 46
assessment xi, 110–23
   of pupils 115
   by teachers 130
assessor: mentor as 48
assumptions: by student-teachers 68–9
attitudes: about teaching, students' 19
availability: of mentor 46
awareness: forced 134
   of how and why we teach 125–9
   lack of 120
   of progress, as a teacher 126
   see also critical awareness;
      self-awareness

behaviour: and mathematics 36
   by teacher 77
   see also control
beliefs: about teaching, students' 19,
   113–16
   in teaching mathematics 29–40
bias: and equal opportunities 103
brainstorming: in lesson planning 69, 80

calculation: mental methods of 91–3
challenging student-teachers' awareness
   16, 17
   in development thinking 22
classroom: activities, lesson planning
   around 21
   complexity of 20
   critical incidents in 52–64
   enquiry 136
   equal opportunities in 97, 98–104
   expectations in 52
   experiences, particular and mentor
      23
   interactions in 20
   management 16, 115
   observation, feedback from 48
   reflection in 137–8
   skills 14
   videotaping, use of 132–3
   see also control: in classroom
collaboration: between subjects 106
   with colleagues 124
   see also co-mentoring
co-mentoring 124, 129–33
   departmental agendas 132–3
   external agendas 129–30
   shared agendas 130–1
   whole school agendas 131–2
commitment: to development 128
   to teaching 121
communication skills, interpersonal: of
   mentor 50
confidence: building 7, 21, 48
   with mathematics 36
constructivism 32–3, 35
   as theory of learning 61
content: in lesson planning 70

control: in classroom 84, 117
  objective, in lesson 71, 73–6
counselling 117
critical analysis: in reflective action 135,
  137
critical awareness: development of 87
critical friend 47–9
  and lesson planning 76
  in mentoring role 117
  mentor's need for 127
critical friendship 127, 128
critical incidents x, 47, 79, 86, 91
  definition 53, 54
  focus on 60
  noticing and recording 55–8, 61
  and reflective practice 52–64
  use of 58–62
critical reflection: on teaching
  experience 118
criticism: by students 7
cross-curricular objective: of lesson 71
  in mathematics teaching 96, 104–7,
  115
curriculum, mathematical xi, 17, 42
  choices in 83–4
  criticism of 105
  interpretation of 83–95
  topic, alternative appoaches to 87–91
  see also National Curriculum

debate, chaired 79
debriefing 15, 16
discipline 7
  and mathematics 36
  poor 76
  see also control
discussion: and National Curriculum 86
  need for, on teaching methods 6–7
  and questioning 90–1
displays: mathematics 131

education: versus training ix
encouragement: from fellow professional
  42–5
enthusiasm: of teacher 3–4
equal opportunities ix, xi
  in mathematics teaching 96–104, 115
ethnic background: and equal
  opportunities 99
evaluation 110–23
  beliefs, values and attitudes 113–16
  generalized 111
  guidelines for 111–12
  lesson 78–80

planning for 65, 112–13, 114–15
  process 110–18
  profiles 112
  purposes of 110–11
evaluator: mentor as 48
expectations: and children's learning 52
  of student-teachers 47–8
experience: in teaching 125
experiences, mathematical 21
  for pupils, planning for 65–6
  range and quality 42
experiential learning 25–6
  cyclic stages 26
experimentation: by student-teacher 5–6
expert: 'mantle of', use in teaching
  135–6

failure: of student-teacher 121–2
fallibilism 32, 35
flexibility: in lesson styles 73
  in models of learning 36
  of pupils 36
focuses of attention, self 18–20
  developing teaching expertise 21–3
  teaching skills 20–1
formalism 32, 35

gatekeeper: mentor as 49–50
gender 118–19
  and equal opportunities 99, 100
girls: under achievement in mathematics
  vii, 99
group work 30–1, 38, 79, 115
guide: mentor as 3, 49–50

HE tutors: experience of 24, 25
holding: as supportive role 4–5, 6
holist mode of learning 35

ideas: entrenched, and critical incidents
  54
immaturity: of students 117
inadequacy: feelings of, of
  student-teachers 124
induction programme: for
  student-teachers 50
inner mentor xi, 125
INSET: IT, Initial Teacher Education and
  Inservice Education for Teachers
  130
  days 131
interpretation: of teaching methods
  30–1
intervention: between teachers 10

interviews 53
  techniques of 61
investigational approach 115
isolation: in teaching 13

journal: *see* log

knowledge-in-action 24, 62
knowledge, teachers: tacit 27

language: choice of 57
  and multiple meanings, in critical
    incidents 57
  problem of 60
learning: experiences, for all children
    101
  modes of 35
  objectives 20
lesson evaluation 67, 78–80, 111, 115
  sacrifice of 21
lesson experiences 65–6
lesson plan: important aspects of 67
lesson planning x, 10, 11, 31, 65–82
  around classroom activities 21
  difficulties of 67
  by mentor, discussion of 20
  shared reflection on 66
lesson, observed: and National
    Curriculum 84–7
lesson styles 68–70
  taking risks with 73
letting go: of student-teacher 5–6
liaison: with HE tutors 50
listening 6
  atmosphere, need for, in teaching 3
  role of mentor, as friend 46–7
log: for evaluation 112
  as resource 55
  use of, for critical incidents 55–8
logicism 32, 35
low-achievers: needs of 43, 44

mathematical objectives: of lesson 71
mathematics: common processes in 10
  definition 34
  department, philosophy of, and
    National Curriculum 84
  learning in order 11
  nature of, and mentoring 29
  pupils' perceptions of 106
  uses, in different contexts 105–6,
    115
  value of mentoring 10–12
  and Western culture 100

mathematics teaching: barriers to
    learning 25
  development of 137–8
  reasons for 97
  variety in 24, 29
meetings, departmental: structure of 132
mentor: articulation of ideas 38–9
  communication with tutor 57
  difficulties in becoming 27
  enthusiasm of 3–4
  as guide 3, 49–50, 61
  influence on students 98
  new 124
  personal development 4
  professional development of 124, 126,
    129, 132
  responsibilities, as critical friend 128
  responsibilities, in evaluation 118–21
  roles of 3–4, 5, 41–51, 57
  trust in 4, 80, 102
  see also inner mentor
mentoring: development of process of
    124–5
  environment 6–10
  influence of, on mentor 1–2, 11–12,
    20
  limits on 4–5
  listening atmosphere 3
  mathematics compared to other
    subjects 39–40
  practice of x
  roles and relationships in x, 3–4, 5,
    41–51, 102, 103, 133
  value in mathematics 10–12
  see also co-mentoring
messages 53
microcomputer: use of, in learning
    mathematics 93–4
MSO, Mutual Support and Observation
    131–2
multicultures: and equal opportunities
    xi, 99

National Curriculum: interpretation of
    83–95
  and lesson planning 65–6
  Non-Statutory Guidance 92, 95
novice teachers ix

objectives: for lesson planning 70–3
observation: active role of 76
  extended 19
  planning for 65, 76–7
  and self-awareness 102

semiformal 7
value of 45
see also classroom observation
offering advice: to student 16
ongoing process: of learning to teach 1
organization: of classroom 115

parental expectations: in mathematics
101
pastoral work 115
performance 53
personal development: of teacher 4
PGCE, Post-Graduate Certificate of
Education viii
philosophy: of mathematics 31–2, 97
physical disability: and equal
opportunities 99
planning, by student-teacher 65–82
process of 68–76
content 70
control 73–6
objectives 70–3
styles of 68–70
purposes of 65–6
see also lesson plans
Platonism 32
power: of mathematics, for
communication vii
preferences: in mathematics 35
preparation: of lessons 115
see also lesson planning
probing student-teachers' thinking 17
and development teaching 22
process skills 94
professional development: *see under*
mentor
professional practice: aspects of 44–5
professional qualities 115
profiles: of evaluation 112
see also log
pupils: awareness of concepts 88
behaviour, with student-teachers 51
different perspectives from teachers
33–4
mixed ability 43, 45
and modes of learning 35–6
objectives 71–2
and reflective practice 138
student-teachers' relationship with
115
views on student-teachers 119
ways to approach 11–12, 15
work, discussion of 132
Pythagorean theorem 33

questioning: in critical friendship 128–9
in lesson evaluation 78
and National Curriculum 86, 87, 90

race: and equal opportunities 99
recording: critical incidents 55–8
reflection-in-action 62, 133–34
reflective focus: on teaching 22
reflective practice x, 24, 26, 52–64
in classroom 137–8
in co-mentoring 129–33
the inner mentor 133–7
meaning of 62
sequence of stages 134–5
reflective practitioner 62
and planning for observation 77
teachers as 138
reflective skills, and critical incidents
52–64
reflective thinking 134
relationships: in mentoring process x,
3–4, 41–51
research: action-, 63–4, 136–7
aim of 63
dissemination 136
internal, by mentor 136–7
relevance of 136
resources 42, 43
responsibility, as critical friend:
to other teachers 128
to student teachers 128
roles: in mentoring process x, 3–4, 5,
41–51, 57, 133

school-based initial teacher education
23, 25
school issues: and co-mentoring 131
school policy: on equal opportunities
and cross-curricular links 96
school social setting 48
self-awareness: and equal opportunities
101–3
of progress, as teacher 126
self-criticism: lack of 120
self-evaluative capabilities 99, 123
development of 111
need for 48
see also evaluation
sensitivity: lack of 120
serialist mode of learning 35
shadowing: in cross-curricular
observation 104–5
sine and cosine functions 88–9

skills, teaching: acquiring and using 14
  focusing on 20–1
  general 115
social objective: of lesson 71
staff appraisal 129–30
statistics: in cross-curricular links 106
  and equal opportunities 101
status: of student-teachers 51
stress: reducing 6
structure: and discussion meetings 6
student-teachers: activities for 39
  criticism by 7
  expectations of 47
  focus on 18–20
  introduction by mentor 49
  narrow content-based view of
    mathematics 95
  trust in mentor 4, 80
  using knowledge of, by other teachers
    133
styles: of lesson plans 68–70
support: of fellow professional 42–5
  of mentor, as critic 47–9
syllabus: changes in 130

targets: achievable 111
tasks 53
teacher education ix
  school-based 23
teachers viii
  articulation of ideas 38–9
  assessment 130
  behaviour 77
  input, at meetings 132
  objectives, in lessons 72–3
  personal style, development of 45
  as reflective practitioners 138
  response to unexpected 88
  role of 36
  see also mentors
teacher training ix

teaching: approaches, comparison of
    115
  definition of 2–3
  developing, focus on 21–2
  experience 118
  good, meaning of 3
  learning to, and mentor support
    13–28
  reasons for 97, 107
  reflection on 6–7, 11–12, 20
  styles 42, 120
    contrasting 105
  suitability for 111, 119
  techniques, advice on 9
  see also skills, teaching
techniques, teaching: acquiring and
    using 14
ticking work 53
training: versus education ix
trust: need for, in mentors 4, 80, 102
tutors viii
  communication with mentor 57
  role of 57

understanding: mathematics 8, 58, 59
  teacher's, about children 58–9

values: and evaluation 113–16
video, use of: classroom, in
    co-mentoring 132–3
  for critical incidents 56
  to record student lesson 20–1
views, of mathematics 31–2, 40
  differing 34, 36
  discussion on 34–6
  effects, in classroom 36–8
  sharing 35–6

web diagram: in lesson planning 69
Western culture: and mathematics 100
working together 51